To Mr & Mrs Albert Monroe

To Remember
Old Ascutan Days
with the best wishes
of the Friend
M.W. Nelson

TINKER AND THINKER
JOHN BUNYAN
1628-1688

by
William Hamilton Nelson

Drawn by Ralph Chessé

CHRISTIAN CLIMBS THE HILL OF DIFFICULTY

TINKER AND THINKER
JOHN BUNYAN

1628-1688

by

William Hamilton Nelson

WILLETT, CLARK & COLBY
440 South Dearborn Street, Chicago
200 Fifth Avenue, New York

1928

CONTENTS

DRAWINGS BY

RALPH CHESSÉ
San Francisco

A Personal Word

From the Author to His Readers.

A little over thirty years ago, when I was a boy of sixteen, I walked into a second-hand book store in the French quarter of New Orleans, on Rue Chartres near Canal, and saw a large table filled with second-hand books which bore the enticing legend, "Any book on this table 20 cents." This just about fitted my pocketbook. Even at that age it was just as hard for me to pass a second-hand book store as it was for some folks to pass a saloon; so I began browsing around and picked up a book which had a reference to Vanity Fair in it. I said to myself, "This must be something like Thackeray; it ought to be good."

Well, the book was good, but it was nothing like Thackeray. It was different from anything I had read. I wondered about it. It was not one of those Keys to the Bible which are so numerous in this country. As the French say, "on the contrary," the Bible was the key to this book. I had never read the Bible, and so in order not to lose my twenty cents, I went around to another second-hand book store and bought a second-hand Bible for thirty-five cents.

Although only sixteen I was making my own living at the time, working hard all day, and had leisure to read only at night. I looked up every Scripture reference in this second-hand book and it took me quite a while to read it. But when I got through reading the book I had been completely revolutionized. In the language of both books, I had been "born again." It changed the whole current of my life. I started in with a man named Christian; ran with him from the City of Destruction; fell with him in the Slough of Despond; went into the House of the Interpreter with him; went through the Wicket Gate, and felt my burden roll away at the foot of the cross; and I am still traveling the road he trod this side of the river.

The name of that book is Pilgrim's Progress. It was printed 250 years ago, July, 1678. It has done the same thing all over the world that it did for me. Next to the Bible it is translated into more languages than any book ever written. For nearly a generation I have been saturated with the book; my life has been colored by it, and more than colored—it has been made by it. You can thus understand my zeal in sending forth this book as a tribute to the author of Pilgrim's Progress. Bunyan did a great deal for me; he can do the same for you. Get a copy of Pilgrim's Progress, or Grace Abounding or The Holy War. "Read, mark, learn and inwardly digest," and the result will be that you will walk in newness of life with Bunyan's Lord. And this new life is worth everything.

WILLIAM HAMILTON NELSON.

San Francisco.
1928

TINKER AND THINKER:
JOHN BUNYAN

The Tinker and His Times

Here's the story of a man; a man who believed something; believed something vital; believed something which touches every man to the very center, and which affects him at every turn of the road; the story of a man who struggled with those elemental mysteries of life more graphically than anything ever written in a Greek tragedy.

This man believed something in an age when it was not easy to believe. He believed it against the edict of one of the cruelest and most despotic of the Stuarts—Charles the Second—who ruled England at times with a rod of iron. He believed what he believed in spite of acts of Parliament; he believed in spite of judges, jails and all the police power. He was willing to give up everything to believe something. On one side of the scale he put a wife and four children whom he loved devotedly, a loving home, his business, his friends, and his health. On the other side he put his conscience and his duty to God and it outweighed all the rest.

In order to get you to know this man better and to get that elusive thing called "color," which is so necessary to our understanding, I am going to do the thing that should be done, that *must* be done in painting a picture of this man: I am going to study him in connection with his times. We need men like that right now, and I am writing with the prayer that what is said here may help us to get that type of man; so let's go along together.

Bunyan's Boyhood in Tempestuous Seventeenth Century Days

John Bunyan was born in November, 1628, three hundred years ago, at Elstow, one mile from the market town of Bedford, England. This is what is called the English Midlands, and lies between the River Trent and the Bedfordshire Ouse. His father, Thomas Bunyan, had him baptized in the Elstow church, according to the parish register, on the 30th of November, 1628. You would be interested to study this old register which shows that his father was baptized on the 24th of February, 1603, and that his name was spelled "Thomas Bunyon." Then, when he was married in 1627 to Margaret Bentley, his name was spelled on the same register "Bonnionn," and when John was baptized, just a year later, they followed the spelling "Bonnionn." Years before the Bunyans came over from Normandy to England, and later settled in Bedfordshire. As early as 1199 they came to Elstow. The English farmers do not move around much, and everything of any importance that happened to John Bunyan happened right around there.

Three years before Bunyan was born—and this is important—Charles the First came to the English throne. His father, James the First, who had the Bible translated, spent most of his time promulgating the now outworn doctrine of the divine right of kings. There was nothing in the English constitution responsible for this notion, but James said that he got it directly from God, always failing, however, to produce a certificate of copyright signed by the Almighty. But as he modestly expressed it, comparing himself to

Omnipotence, "As it is atheism and blasphemy to dispute what God can do, so it is presumption and a high contempt in a subject to dispute what a king can do." This was directed especially at the Puritans of whom he said, "I will make them conform or I will harry them out of the land."

Charles was not as strong as his father, but he had all of his father's absurd notions and none of his good ideas. He made two mistakes right off. He retained the Duke of Buckingham, his father's favorite, as his chief advisor, though nobody had any confidence in the Duke; and soon after Charles took the throne he married Henrietta Maria, a French Catholic princess, who was very extravagant. I am quite sure that this French lady has never been given the proper credit for the way her extravagance influenced English history. It led to the downfall of the divine right of kings, and helped, indirectly, to make John Bunyan.

The year Bunyan was born, just a few months before his birth, June 1628, the Petition of Right was presented by the Lords, spiritual and temporal, and the Commons. This petition was considered dangerous and explosive in that day, but today it only causes us to smile to think that they had to get up a petition on anything of the sort. The petition merely asked the king to stop grafting, in that henceforth no person would be compelled to make loans to him against his will, and no man should be imprisoned, disinherited nor put to death without being brought to answer by the due process of law. Reasonable enough; but Charles felt terribly insulted when it was presented and refused to sign it at first. Now wasn't this a nice age to throw a helpless baby into?

It is likely that Bunyan never read a book of history in his life, but there was a lot of interesting history being made fresh every day when he came on the scene. In the early part of the seventeenth century there was more in a day than just morning, noon and night, as you shall see. Sometimes, and really quite often, there were what Lord Tennyson called, speaking of the hectic reign of an English queen, "spacious days."

Thomas Bunyan had a large family of children, the poor man's only heritage in that day—and this—and the problem of getting three meals a day for hungry and growing children pushed all other thoughts to the back of his head. Bunyan himself said, speaking of his family and

2

their standing as tinkers, that they were looked
upon by the people of England at that time as
"the meanest and most despised of all families
of the land." However, this may be in reverse
English—just as a man often calls himself "the
chief of sinners"—but it is a pleasant rebound
from the usual indoor occupation of bragging on
families.

Bunyan said that he never went to school to
Aristotle or to Plato, but was brought up in his
father's house (they were not gypsies) in a very
mean condition among a company of poor coun-
trymen. There were very few schools in England
at that time—there were none in Elstow—but
there was one in Bedford, a mile away, endowed
by the generosity of a good man, and Bunyan
walked the mile from Elstow to Bedford and
got a smattering of the three R's.

Wonderful Dreams

When Bunyan was nine years of age he
began to have some wonderful dreams. The
intellectual electricity which was in the air set his
mind to working, and he began to be concerned,
not about politics, but about his own soul. There

was in him a tendency toward evil, and yet there was this innate religious nature at work like a ferment, which resulted in these dreams. He saw evil spirits in all sorts of hideous shapes, and fiends blowing long incandescent flames out of their mouths. Often the heavens were on fire and burning up like a house, and all the thunder ever manufactured was at work; and in the midst of it all an archangel flying through heaven, sounding his trumpet; and seated on a throne in the east sat a Glorious One like the bright and morning star. This of course was the end of the world to his mind, and he did what we all would have done, boy or man: he fell on his knees and prayed, "O Lord, have mercy on me. What shall I do? The day of judgment is come and I am not prepared."

In another dream, when he was out having a roystering good time, an earthquake cracked the world, and out of the canyons came blood and fire, and men dressed up in flaming globes, while devils laughed at their torments. The earth began to sink under him, the flames licked near him, but when he began to think he was about to perish, One in shining raiment descended and plucked him as a brand from the burning. In the daytime also, like Joan of Arc, he had visions and heard voices.

It is a good thing for John Bunyan that he lived when he did, for if he had lived today all sorts of folks would be "projekin" with him, as the old Southern negroes say. He would be subjected to Binet tests and whatnot. Supposedly superior people today would laugh at that strange, earnest-minded boy for some of the things he did. They would want to cure him, sending him to a nerve specialist or a psychiatrist; or they would have him psycho-analyzed—and spoil him.

As far as I am concerned I am quite sure that God was dealing with that boy's soul. Those dreams and that perfervid imagination came in handy later on for his immortal book, for the Pilgrim's Progress was written under the similitude of a dream, and with the aid of an imagination which worked for the blessing of the world.

Bunyan at Twelve
Royalist and Roundhead Strife

In 1640, when Bunyan was twelve years of age, the Earl of Strafford became prime minister, and by means of the Star Chamber sought to make Charles absolute and establish a complete despotism. Archbishop Laud, who soon became head of the Established Church, worked with Strafford through the High Commission court. These religio-politico twins furnished a horrible example for the union of Church and State: The Star Chamber put in prison those who refused the king's demands for money, and the High Commission punished those who could not conform to the Established Church.

The next little piece of graft the king tried to work was known as Ship Money. This tax was to furnish equipment for the standing army —to guarantee that the king might keep his crown on straight. The pretext was the flimsiest in that it was to protect the English coast from Algerian pirates—he overlooked the Swiss navy. This Ship Money tax started a farmer named John Hampden going, for they taxed the inland towns as well as the seacoast. Hampden and another farmer named Oliver Cromwell, his cousin, felt that they had stood about all they could. They got on a boat in the Thames all set to emigrate to the American colonies, but were stopped by the king's orders. It is safe to say

that Charles regretted his action at least ten
thousand times in the balance of his worthless
life, for Hampden and Cromwell started a revo-
lution which cost the king his head.

In 1640 Bunyan was twelve years of age.
The Long Parliament met that year, and was
composed of sure-enough Englishmen. We can
think whatever we please about the English, but
in spite of kings and headsmen and prison, the
urge for liberty is strong within them. Parliament sentenced Strafford to execution for his
oppression. The king refused to sign the death
warrant, but the people were so clamorous that
he had to do it.

They next got Laud for attempting to,
overthrow the Protestant religion; they abolished
the Star Chamber and the High Commission
court, and they passed a bill requiring Parliament to be summoned once in three years. They
followed this by drawing up the Grand Remon-
strance, in which they held up to the light the
faults of the king's government, and their dis-
trust in his policy. Then they enacted a law
forbidding "the dissolution of the present Parliament except by its own consent." And not
only that, but they were on the verge of drawing

up a bill of impeachment against the queen for having conspired with the Roman Catholics and the Irish to destroy the liberties of the country.

Charles knew that they had the goods on his wife, and so he was driven to extremities. He requested the House of Commons to give up the five members who headed the impeachment proceedings, on the charge of high treason, which they refused to do. The queen taunted him: "Go, coward; pull those rogues out by the ears." He went with an armed force, but the members were in hiding. He asked the Speaker of the House where they were, but this servile tool, kneeling before the king, was so afraid of Parliament that he could only say, "I neither see nor speak but by command of the House." There was no standing army in England in those days, but there was a body of militia in every county and in every large town, and these were occasionally called out to drill. The king started the civil war by leaving London and going to Nottingham to get an army to attack Parliament.

England was pretty well divided by an irregular line running as far north as York, which cut the country almost in two; the east half, including London, going with Parliament, and the west half lining up with the king. The nobility, the clergy and the country gentlemen, known as cavaliers because they were fine horsemen, were in the king's army, while the petty tradesmen and small farmers were with Parliament. Both sides had to make great sacrifices to carry on the war. The grasping queen was compelled to sell her crown jewels, illustrating Don Quixote's proverb, "Coveteousness bursts the bag."

The first battle between the Royalists and Roundheads was fought at Edgehill, in 1642, and was a victory for the king. Each of the rival armies carried a printing press with it, and waged furious battle in type against the other. The whole country was sown down with pamphlets, about thirty thousand of them coming out in a few years, discussing every conceivable religious and political question.

When Bunyan Was Only Fourteen

When the war broke in '42 Bunyan was only fourteen years of age. The visions and voices had ceased temporarily. He says of this period that

God left him to himself, and delivered him over
to his wicked imagination. He fell into all kinds
of petty vice, such as poaching, ringing church
bells, and the severer vice of swearing. This last
was Bunyan's besetting sin, and stayed with him
until he was a grown man. He was morally
clean, for in later years he said with a good deal
of emphasis, that no matter what else he did he
had never gone astray on the vice of uncleanness.

Of course he had high animal spirits as a
boy; he was healthy and vigorous, and he was
always into something. Once or twice he nearly
lost his life. He fell in a creek that led into the
sea, and was on the point of drowning; and
another time he fell in the River Ouse, and
nearly met a watery grave. He says of himself
in his "History of Mr. Badman," "Though I
could sin with delight and ease, and take pleasure
in the villainies of my companions, even then if
I saw wicked things done by them that professed
goodness it would make my spirit tremble. Once,
when I was in the height of my vanity, hearing
one swear who was reckoned a religious man, it
made my heart to ache."

When Bunyan was sixteen his mother died,
and in another month his sister Margaret passed

away. A month after that his father married
again. John felt this very keenly, and it is
believed that this strong-minded, independent
boy left home and started out in business on his
own account, mending pots and pans. Bedfordshire was in Parliamentary territory. The feeling against the king was almost unanimous there,
and when an order came to Bedford for a company of soldiers for the Parliamentary army
Bunyan was drafted. The roster rolls of New-
port Pagnell, discovered a few years ago, show
that Bunyan served under Sir Samuel Lake, the
original of Butler's Hudibras. He was probably
close to seventeen then.

Bunyan — the Soldier

He was not a militarist; you find only a
meager reference to his army experience in anything he wrote. One thing made an impression
on his mind, and that was an experience that bor-
dered on the religious. He writes these words:
"When I was a soldier I was with others drawn
out to go to such a place to besiege it. But when
I was just ready to go one of the company
desired to go in my room. Coming to the siege

as he stood sentinel he was shot in the heart with a musket ball, and died." However, as much as he refrained from any boasting of his own part in the war it is certain that Bunyan got some of his material for the "Holy War" out of this brief army experience of one year. He was born with literary talent; it was a gift, and quite naturally all was grist that came to his mill.

Political and Religious Turmoil
Sweeps on

When Bunyan was seventeen the war came to an end, Cromwell putting the finishing touches to the affair when he cleaned up all north England by his smashing victory at Naseby in 1645. After the fight, papers belonging to the king were picked up on the battle field which proved that Charles intended betraying those who were negotiating with him for peace and that he was planning to bring foreign troops to England. The army ruled England after Charles was taken prisoner.

In 1648 Charles fled to the Isle of Wight, came back early in January, '49, raised an army, and was defeated at the Battle of Preston. On

January 20, 1649, he was brought into court, adjudged guilty of being an enemy to the country, and ten days later, on January 30th, he was executed. Soon after that the Commonwealth was established. In less than two months the House of Commons passed the act making England a republic, and the House of Lords was abolished as both "dangerous and useless."

At this time religion was in the air. The Commonwealth or Parliamentary army, especially Oliver Cromwell's "Old Ironsides," was composed of men who could watch as well as pray. "Have faith in God and keep your powder dry," that was their motto. Like the army of Stonewall Jackson, they held numerous prayer meetings. Cromwell said of them, "A lovely company." They were God-fearing men, and neither swore nor gambled. It was an army in which a consecrated corporal could preach to a callous colonel, if such an individual could be found. The common soldiers not only prayed in private, but in public, and got up in the pulpit and preached to the people. The Parliamentary army carried a printing press around with it and when they were not fighting the enemy they were arguing and writing on religion.

Back of the army the civilians, especially the farmers and artisans, were anticipating William Blake, and were trying to make the New Jerusalem come down to the commons of England. The Sabbath was observed with great strictness; the churches were crowded, not once, but three and four times on Sunday; family altars were established, and people prayed around the hearthstone, read the Bible, and discussed sermons. They talked religion on the streets, in the shops, and in the fields. It is said that in that time you might walk through the city of London on a Sunday evening without seeing an idle person, or hearing anything but the voice of prayer or praise from churches and private houses. There were no gambling houses or profane houses; swearing was punished severely. No wonder Bunyan came under severe religious conviction at this time.

Bunyan the Boy
Becomes Bunyan the Man

In 1649, the year of the establishment of the Commonwealth, with John Bradshaw as president, John Milton foreign secretary, Cromwell one of the commanders in chief of the fighting forces, the army was the real power behind the throne, before the throne, on the side of the throne, and for that matter, under it. The safety of the Commonwealth was truly under the shadow of swords. In 1649 Bunyan married. He was working at the tinker's trade at that time. It is interesting to note right here that in 1905 Bunyan's anvil with his name stamped on it and the date 1647, was discovered in a pile of rubbish at St. Neots, near Bedford. Bunyan married a woman, some distance from Elstow, and was very fortunate, for she was an orphan, and had no close friends or relatives. He was lucky again, for she was a poor girl, and it is easy to bring that kind up in the style to which they are accustomed.

Bunyan said they were so poor, both of them, that when they married they had not so much household stuff as a dish or a spoon between them. But she had a dowry far better than silver plate: her father was a godly man, and left a good name and a good influence. Also she brought her husband two books, which changed the whole current of his being. One was called, "The Practice of Piety," and the other,

"The Plain Man's Pathway to Heaven." Like
Paola and Francesca, though with a pure love,
they used to turn the leaves of the open book
together. Much of their happiness consisted in
sitting by the fire and reading to each other after
the hard day's work was done.

"The Plain Man's Pathway" influenced
Bunyan a great deal, and some critics say that
much of it filtered into his mind and came out in
"The Life and Death of Mr. Badman," published thirty years later. "The Pathway" is a
dialogue between four people on the question of
the soul's salvation. It was written in simple
English and had some choice epigrams in it. Consider these: "A fool's bolt is soon shot," and "He
that never doubted never believed." Of course
everything that comes up in a man's religious
life is discussed, and it borders on casuistry in
ethical questions. The reading of this book stirred
Bunyan until, like Mr. Attentive in the book, he
was greatly concerned for his soul.

Four Years of Sense of Sin

There were times in Bunyan's life when his
sense of sin was like a volcano. One morning I

stood on the top of a building in Red Bluff, California, and saw Mount Lassen, the only live volcano in the United States, blowing its head off. There was a thick volume of black smoke rising out of the crater, and then mushrooming over the top. Occasionally the black smoke was cut by livid flames of fire, just as a golden knife will cut a dark garment. The next day Lassen was dormant, and was that way for nearly a year, when it broke out again. Bunyan had spells of conviction, and then his religious nature would be dormant, and then he would become anxious again.

John's despair in these periods of conviction reached to the very bowels of the earth. Out of the depths he cried unto God; he struggled with weepings in the miry clay and the horrible pit, his Slough of Despond. After his marriage his despair reached the deepest depths. We are not trying to be facetious; we are simply recording a fact of history. Bunyan had the exceedingly good fortune of being happily married. His wife was desperately in love with him, but earthly love could not satisfy the craving of a heart which was blindly groping after God. Like the Psalmist he could say, "My heart and my flesh crieth out for

God, for the living God. When shall I come and appear before God?"

Like his own Christian his burden was breaking his back and his heart. He was in Doubting Castle kept by Giant Despair, and he believed there was no hope for him. He would be damned eternally; his day of grace had passed; in fact he thought it had passed for all the people in that part of England who were not Jews. He tried to believe he had Jewish blood in him, but the family tree was against him. He got it into his head that he had committed the unpardonable sin, and a well-meaning but misguided old man, to whom he went for advice, told him that he was sure he had. He heard voices begging him to betray his Lord, and he would cry out audibly, "Not for ten thousand worlds." But then the voices of the fiends would become more insistent than ever, and finally the only way he could get rid of them was to say, "Let him (Christ) go if he will." He believed that he had thus sold his Christ, and his despair almost drove him frantic.

Bunyan's work, "Grace Abounding to the Chief of Sinners" is a spiritual autobiography, and he lays his soul bare in it. The years from

3

Drawn by Ralph Chessé

CHRISTIAN BATTLES APOLLYON

'49 to '53 were perhaps the most dramatic, dynamic and terrible in his life. Most of the time he was not only at Mount Sinai amid the thunders and lightnings and the terrible voices, but he was walking down the main street of hell. You will remember in the Pilgrim's Progress one of the most dramatic incidents is where Christian in the Valley of Humiliation fights with the fiend Apollyon. According to Bunyan, this monster was hideous to behold. He was clothed with scales like a fish, had wings like a dragon, feet like a bear, and out of his belly came fire and smoke, and his mouth was the mouth of a lion. You will remember that in the conflict this monster threw darts as thick as hail, and wounded Christian in the head, the hand and the foot. The combat was sore, and lasted until Christian grew faint because of his many wounds. I imagine that when Bunyan was writing the Progress he turned often to these memorable four years.

Bunyan was trying to raise himself by his boot-straps religiously. He began to lop off this sin and put on that virtue. He began to attend church twice on Sunday and to quit poaching. One Sunday after having heard a sermon on Sabbath-breaking he was out on the village green at Bedford in the afternoon, indulging in his usual game of tip-cat, in some ways the great, great grand-father of baseball. He was just about to hit the ball when he seemed to hear a voice in the heavens calling unto him saying, "Wilt thou leave thy sins and go to heaven, or keep thy sins and go to hell?" So he quit playing tip-cat.

Also a favorite sport of that time which troubled his conscience was ringing bells in the tower of Elstow church. He gave this practice up after a struggle. He tells us about it in his own quaint way: "I would go to the steeplehouse and look on, though I durst not ring, . . . but quickly after I began to think how if one of the bells should fall? So after this I would yet go to see them ring, but would not go any farther than the steeple door. But then it came into my head, how if the steeple itself should fall? And this thought . . . did continually so shake my mind that I durst not stand at the steeple door any longer, but was forced to flee for fear the steeple should fall upon my head." So Bunyan quit ringing church bells, but instead of trimming the branches he realized later that he should have been laying his ax at the root of the tree.

One day he was in Bedford looking for pots and kettles to mend, and he stood outside of a little shop to talk to the proprietor. He was so in the habit of swearing that he seemed to do it automatically. A woman with a notorious reputation was in the shop, and she told him that she had had a lot of experience, but he was the most ungodly swearer she had ever heard, and that he was enough to spoil all the boys in the town. He said the reproof struck him right between the joints in his armor, and cut him to the quick. That a person of this character should object to his swearing was the limit. He resolved to quit right then.

The "Holy War"
Within Himself

Not long after this he heard some old ladies in Bedford—there were four in the group, I believe—who were sitting out on a doorstep talking about the things of God. He kept in the background where he could not be seen, for he was interested, but he listened in. They were doing what the Methodist folks were to do later: telling their experiences. Experience is the crowning glory of the Christian religion, and it is the one answer to every question. When a man can tell what he has seen and felt he has something that people will listen to. But everything they were saying was over Bunyan's head. Religion to him was like a Christmas tree, which you trimmed down and then dolled up, hanging on presents; to them it was like a tree planted by the rivers of water, which brought forth fruit in season; not fruit hung on, but which grew naturally and came from a live center. They talked of the new birth, and this was something new to him. He wanted to know more of it, so he made it a point to talk to some of these good ladies every time he could. They finally became quite interested in him, and directed him to the Rev. John Gifford.

At this time Gifford was rector of St. John's Church in Bedford, although he was a Baptist. This was a strange situation. When the Commonwealth came to power the Episcopal Church was disestablished. The bench of Bishops was abolished, and the dominant churches were the Congregationalists and the Presbyterians. These two large factions were divided, but Cromwell's Toleration Order did much to bring them to-

gether, helping also the smaller non-conformist
bodies, as the Quakers, the Baptists, and others.
This order settled the question of church government, which was the bone of contention, and
allowed each congregation to choose its own minister, and select its own form of church government. The only thing asked was that the government must be satisfied as to the moral and
intellectual efficiency of the man nominated by a
congregation to be its minister.

Practically all of Bedfordshire at this time
was in sympathy with the Commonwealth and
its laws, and the majority that took charge of
St. John's Church called Gifford to be its rector.
The Rev. John Gifford had a war experience
himself. He had been drafted into the Royalist
army in the west of England, was taken prisoner
by the Roundheads and sentenced to be hanged.
His sister came to visit him, and found out that
she could effect his escape. He got out in the
night, went into hiding, and after the war was
over came to Bedford to settle down. He became
a quack doctor, but falling under religious conviction was converted and became a pastor of the
church in Bedford. Gifford was never a Royalist
at heart, politically or religiously, and after his

conversion he became very zealously independent.
If he was not an orthodox doctor he became an
orthodox preacher, for he filled St. Paul's pre-
scription, "called to be saints." He was called,
"the holy Mr. Gifford," and some think that
Bunyan had him in mind when he drew the
character of Evangelist in the Pilgrim.

In "Grace Abounding" Bunyan says that at
this time he sat under the ministry of holy Mr.
Gifford, "whose doctrine by God's grace was
much for my stability." He said Gifford made
it his business to deliver folk from all that was
false and unsound; exhorting them not to take
things too easily, but to cry mightily to God. No
doubt Bunyan was passing through deep waters
at this time, and Gifford, who believed in being
very thorough, did not minimize the struggle. He
believed that the kingdom of heaven suffered and
the violent took it by force. He was a help to
Bunyan, but for awhile he made Bunyan go
deeper down, just as a pearl diver has to get to
the bottom before he can bring up his treasure.
And he impressed it on Bunyan that he could
help him only up to a certain point; that finally
he had to stand alone. Naked the soul goes up to
God, and naked do we fight our own battles.

I have no doubt but that this experience with Gifford had its effect on the writing of the Pilgrim. Christian fights it out with the fiend Apollyon without anyone whispering directions to him as to how to handle his sword. Gifford did help Bunyan, but it was not the work of a day or a week, for Gifford was not easy on him, or anyone else, when it came to the salvation of the soul, and Bunyan was not easy on himself.

Bunyan said that he was at this time farther than ever from the kingdom. As he expressed it, "As to the act of sinning I was never more tender than now. I durst not take up a pin or a stick though but so big as a straw, for my conscience was now sore and would smart at every touch. I could not tell how to speak my words for fear I should misplace them." He joined the Baptist church, was baptized in the River Ouse, but did not have the assurance that he had passed from death unto life. The experience of all great saints is that the Christian life is not a battle but a war. They may lose a battle but win the war; they may lose a battle, win a battle, and lose the next time; there may be many battles before the issue is settled finally. Bunyan experienced this, and I think that is one of the reasons why he wrote his "Holy War" wherein the battle rages, not once or twice but several times. This is the story of Christian also in the Pilgrim. And so, soon after this baptism the fight was on, and harder than ever.

Bunyan Doubts —
But Battles on

In the "Holy War" that "nimble-Jack" Mr. Unbelief, is the only one who finally makes his escape after all the Diabolians are slain. This is true in the case of every Christian, the last enemy to be destroyed is Doubt. This was Bunyan's doubting time. He doubted whether the holy scriptures were false or true; whether Christ was divine or merely a human being; he even doubted the existence of God. He questioned whether the Koran was not as good as the Bible, and whether Mohammed was not as good as Jesus. The millions of people in the various parts of the world who had never even heard of Christ worried him. He thought of the Jews, Mohammedans, pagans, who all believed in their religion, and he wondered if Christianity was but a "think-so," too?

He even believed he was possessed of the devil, and a whole string of sulphurous blasphemy was poured into his ears. He believed that there was not the slightest chance for him. He thought he heard God saying of him, "This poor, simple wretch doth hanker after Me, as if I had nothing to do but to bestow it on such as he. Poor fool; how art thou deceived. It is not for such as thee to have favor with the Highest." Those were days of great tempest and dark and lowering clouds. "He dwelt in the land of darkness as darkness itself and where the light was as darkness." The Book of Job has been called an epic, and the life of Job approaches tragedy; so it was with the life of Bunyan, who was just as desperately in earnest as the Man of Uz. God is love, and God is light, but for a man who has not been pardoned it is a fearful thing to fall into the hand of the living God, for in the depths of conviction he is a consuming fire. Bunyan could say of his spiritual torment what Job said:

"He teareth me in his wrath who hateth me; he gnasheth upon me with his teeth; mine enemies sharpen their eyes upon me. They have gaped upon me with their mouth; they have smitten me upon the cheek reproachfully; they have gathered themselves together against me. God hath delivered me over to the ungodly, and turned me over into the hands of the wicked. I was at ease, but he hath broken me asunder; he hath also taken me by my neck and shaken me to pieces, and set me up for his mark. His archers compass me round about; he cleaveth my reins asunder, and doth not spare, he poureth out my gall upon the ground. He breaketh me with breach upon breach; he runneth upon me like a giant. My face is foul with weeping, and on mine eyelids is the shadow of death. My breath is corrupt, my days are extinct, the graves are ready for me!"

And yet all the while he followed hard after God. He was trying to rely on the written Word. He had all sorts of tests as to whether he was received of God or not. On one occasion he was walking on the road between Elstow and Bedford, and was thinking of the story of Gideon. You remember Gideon asked God for a sign, and the fleece was wet or dry according to his desire. Bunyan was tempted to ask the Lord to dry up the horseponds, and make some dry places a pool. But then that strain of hard sense which characterized him in latter life came

to the surface for air on this occasion, and he
concluded he had better go behind the hedge and
pray over it first, for he argued that if it did
not come out as he expected he would be
desperate.

Now and then a ray of sunlight burst
through. He was riding in the country, and the
Scripture came into his mind while he was mus-
ing on his wickedness, "He hath made peace
through the blood of his cross." He saw that the
justice of God and his sinful soul could embrace
and kiss each other. He saw Christ in the spirit
on the right hand of the Father pleading for
him. Also at that time, fortunately, Luther's
Preface to the Commentary on Galatians fell
into his hands, so old that it was like to fall to
pieces. He said, "I do prefer this book of Martin
Luther (excepting the Holy Bible) before all
books that ever I have seen as most fit for a
wounded conscience."

He had "gained Christ," as he termed it,
and yet it all seemed too good to be true. Salvation was so precious to him that he could hardly
believe it. An old temptation in a new form
assailed him. He was tempted to sell this most
blessed Christ, to exchange him for the things

of this life. He said that for a year there were days when nothing else was in his mind. He could hardly sleep. The devils were dinning it into his brain, "Sell Christ for this; sell Christ for that; sell him; sell him," and Bunyan would cry out in his agony, "I will not, I will not."

But finally, he must have been thoroughly distracted and brain fevered, for he yielded when worn out: "Let him go if he will." He said he felt like a bird shot from a tree. He got out of bed and went "moping" in the fields at the dead of night. He was a Judas, an Esau; he was worse than both of them put together. Bunyan was in the Valley of the Shadow. You remember in the Pilgrim Christian asked those who had been in the Valley what they had seen. Their reply was, "Seen! Why, the Valley itself, which is as dark as pitch: we also saw there the hobgoblins, satyrs, and dragons of the pit: we heard also in that Valley a continued howling and yelling, as of a people under unutterable misery, who there sat bound in affliction and irons; and over that Valley the discouraging clouds of confusion: Death, also, doth always spread his wings over it. In a word, it is every whit dreadful, being utterly without order."

And then, in the very depths of his despair there was a flash of light. He says, "One day as I was passing into the field, and that too with some dashes on my conscience, fearing lest yet all was not right, suddenly this sentence fell upon my soul, 'Thy righteousness is in heaven.' And methought withal, I saw with the eyes of my soul Jesus Christ at God's right hand; there, I say, was my righteousness; so that wherever I was, or whatever I was doing, God could not say to me, 'He wants my righteousness,' for that was just before him. I also saw, moreover, that it was not my good frame of heart that made my righteousness worse; for my righteousness was Jesus Christ himself, 'the same yesterday, today and for ever.' "

The Chains Fell Off

He says that at this time the chains fell off his legs, he was loosed from his afflictions and irons which had bound his hands, his temptations fled away, and from that time "those dreadful scriptures of God left off to trouble me. Now I went home rejoicing for the grace and love of God. Christ of God is made unto us wisdom and righteousness, and sanctification and redemption. I now lived very sweetly, at peace with God through Christ. Oh, Merciful Christ! Christ! There was nothing but Christ before my eyes."

Political Changes Destined to Affect Bunyan's Life

Right about this time political changes were occurring in England which were destined to affect Bunyan's whole life. They were going to be hard on him physically, and even his fair financial status would be dreadfully disturbed. His family would be hard hit, and he knew it. But the trouble he was called to go through would *make him* mentally and spiritually, and if the thing we are about to relate had not happened it is likely the world would never have known John Bunyan, and Pilgrim's Progress would never have been written.

In 1658 Oliver Cromwell died. We believe in eugenics. It is a great blessing for a child to be well born. We believe that blood will tell, but there is no recipe for genius, and there is no sure means of inheriting outstanding ability. The old miners out in California in the days of '49 used to say, that gold was wherever you found it. It is that way with genius and superabundant mental strength. If you do not believe this just run over the list of great men, and look up their children.

For instance take the case of Oliver Cromwell and Richard Cromwell. You can hate Oliver Cromwell all you please, but he was Old Ironsides himself. If I were an artist and wanted to paint a picture of Strength I would show Cromwell kicking the Rump Parliament out, locking the door of the House of Commons, and putting the key in his pocket. During his reign as Protector, from 1653 to 1658, he not only made England respected all over the world, which the Stuarts had never done, but he made England feared. When he died his son, Richard, came to the throne, and reigned only eight months, pleased beyond measure when the army leaders told him to get out. The job of ruling England was too heavy for "Tumble-down-Dick," and he gladly retired into obscurity, cherishing to the end of his life an old trunk filled with congratulatory addresses and honeyed resolutions which the English knew how to write so

4

well. Tumble-down-Dick's resignation spelled trouble for Bunyan, as we will show.

In 1660 Charles the Second, a refugee in Holland, was invited to return to England and take the throne. He was received at Dover with the wildest enthusiasm. Bonfires were lighted, and it was a continuous round of pleasure all the way from the channel to London. The Stuarts lacked a great deal of being ideal rulers, but they were always strong on one thing, and that was sarcasm. As the boot-lickers of all classes from lords to laborers crowded around the king to tell him how glad they were to see him, and how they were just dying to get him back, he remarked with characteristic Stuart sarcasm, "It must have been my own fault that I did not come back before, for I find no one but declares he is glad to see me."

Charles the Second has been characterized as "one of the most promising, lying, unprincipled, worthless, selfish and corrupting kings that ever sat on the throne of England." The Edinburgh Review said of him that he superseded "the reign of the saints by the reign of strumpets; who was crowned in his youth with the Covenant in his hand, and died with the Host sticking in his throat, after a life spent in dawdling suspense between Hobbism (atheism) and Popery." But Charles knew what he wanted, and he wanted above all things to break down the power of Puritanism which had taken his father's head, and sent him off a wanderer. The first thing he did was to break up the Parliamentary army, but he picked an overlarge "Swiss guard" of 5000 to guard his own precious skin, and to become the nucleus of a standing army which would oppose the Puritans, and, if necessary, "harry them out of the land."

An impartial historian says that the throne was in every way the exact opposite of Cromwell's. Charles had no special love for England, and nothing but hardened cynicism regarding the goodness or virtue of men or women. For twelve years he had been an unwelcome wanderer in Continental Europe, and lived off the largesse thrown him by other sovereigns, as one would cast a collection of choice bones to a hungry dog. He considered he had had a hard time of it, and now he was in for a reign of pleasure. A writer of that time says he was "a good human, but a hard-hearted voluptuary." The initial letters of the names of his chief advisors, five in number, Clifford, Ashley, Buckingham, Arlington and Lauderdale, spelled out the word "cabal," an underground political "ring," which was brought into being by the new king. Charles' choice companions were a bunch of libertines, and the royal palace became really a harem.

Puritanism may have gone to the extreme in some petty matters regulating social conduct, but the so-called Restoration went the other way, and, encouraged by the example of the king and court, the flood of looseness was like that tall dam which broke in the St. Francis Canyon in California recently and wiped out all of the surrounding country. Folks just tried to see how bad they could be. They were not only after amusement but in some cases life became an orgy; this was especially true of the higher classes. The brute appeared under the thin veneering of civilization; the Anglo-Saxon cannot disguise it.

You will recall that it was only three years after Charles came to the throne when Samuel Butler published his Hudibras, which was applauded to the echo at that time, and which was thought would live forever. The Puritans, headed by Bunyan's old commander, Sir Thomas

Lake, who was Hudibras himself, were put in a poetic pillory, and the opinion of the so-called upper classes of that time was that the only thing a Puritan head was good for was to serve as a target for mud balls. However, nobody that we know of ever celebrated any of the anniversaries of the publication of the Hudibras, while Pilgrim's Progress is world-wide honored three hundred years after the birth of its author.

Before we leave the question of the reaction from Puritanism we should note this from Pepys' diary (written in that time, and by no Puritan): "there were festivities in which lords and ladies smeared each other's faces with candle grease and soot 'till most of us were like devils." It was the fashion to swear, to relate scandalous adventures, to get drunk, to prate against the preachers and Scripture, and to gamble. There is much more in Pepys telling of bestial and unnatural vices which we cannot name here. A fairly conservative authority of that time says that the Restoration brought with it the throwing off of every profession of virtue, and ended in illicit entertainments and sottish drunkenness which overspread not only England but Scotland and Ireland. The whole force of administration was put to work like a well oiled machine to demoralize the people.

The first thing that Charles did was to punish the members of the High Court of Justice which had sent his father to the block. Ten were executed; nineteen imprisoned for life; a good many others had gone to America, and others escaped soon afterwards. Our New England became a refuge from the royal wrath.

Hanging Dead Bodies

Then Charles was guilty of the puerile act of digging up the bodies of Oliver Cromwell, Ireton, Bradshaw and Pride, taking them from their graves in Westminster Abbey, and hanging them in chains at Tyburn, which, as you know, is near the entrance to Hyde Park, London, and is now the religious, political and social ganglion of the nation as far as the common people are concerned. Here anybody with a theory and a soap box, can talk his head off, and engage to the fullest in his right of free speech. It seems a little ironic to have hung (especially after they were dead) people who fought in the cause of human liberty, at a place like this; but the law of poetic justice is always at work in the world, and seems to take delight in playing tricks on royal boneheads — as time has played the trick on Charles the Second. The next thing Charles did was to call a new Parliament, and pass laws establishing Episcopacy over all the realm.

The Lay Preacher and His Rocky Road

Bunyan was a lay preacher by this time. Soon after joining the Baptist church in Bedford in 1653 his wonderful gifts and graces were manifest. Not that he was perfect or had already attained thereto, for Jordan is a hard road to travel, and Bunyan had some rock roads and the Hill Difficulty still to negotiate. But he had had a wonderful experience; like Dante, he was the man who had seen hell, and he had done more than take a casual look at it. He had seen every inch of that highly advertised place where nobody cares to go, and had felt things few folks ever feel. He was drafted into the Parliamentary army, and he was drafted into the preaching army. He was drafted not because he did not want to preach but because he felt he was not good enough. But when the call came from the brethren of the local church he obeyed, and promised to do his best.

But Bunyan was the kind of a man who wanted bedrock for a foundation, and an inward assurance without the shade of a doubt in it. You will recall in the Pilgrim that one of the men he has no use for is Ignorance. One of the quaint sub-heads he wrote when Ignorance argues with Hopeful and Christian is, "Ignorance jangles with them." Bunyan wanted no jangling; nothing but a sure foundation would do. I imagine that when he as a tinker repaired a pot it was repaired right. He might have written these lines:

"If I were a cobbler it would be my pride
The best of all cobblers to be;
If I were a tinker no tinker beside
Should mend an old kettle like me."

If he had been an engineer he would have built on nothing except the solid rock; if he had built a bridge, a light-house, or a dam, it would have stayed built. Right at this point of preaching, without full assurance, Bunyan reminds us of another John—Wesley. It will be recalled that Wesley came over to Georgia from Eng-

land to preach, without very much assurance in
his own soul. For several years he went through
the motions and read the ritual, but when he met
the leader of the Moravian community in Savan-
nah, and was asked if he had the Witness within
himself, and if the Spirit of God bore witness
with his spirit, he could not answer.

Bunyan preached for five years, and at the
end of that time this is what he said: "I fulfilled
with great sense: for the terrors of the law, and
guilt for my transgressions lay heavy upon my
conscience. I preached what I felt, what smart-
ingly I did feel, even that, under which my poor
soul did groan and tremble to astonishment.
Indeed I have been as one sent to them from the
dead. I went myself in chains to preach to them
in chains; and carried that fire in my own conscience; that I persuaded them to be aware of. I
can truly say, that when I have been to preach I
have gone full of Guilt and Terror to the pulpit
door; and then it hath been taken off, and I have
been at liberty in my mind until I have done my
work; and then immediately, even before I
could get down the pulpit stairs, I have been as
bad as I was before. Yet God carried me on;

but surely with a strong hand, for neither guilt nor hell could take me off my work."

There was one thing about Bunyan's preaching, however; he took it to the folks, and he oxygized it. He was out in the open air, in front of the town hall, on the commons, in the woods— everywhere; and he wasn't making a living out of it, either. He was putting good metal for bad in pots and pans in the daytime, and metal into men's souls at night, and several times on Sunday. The political disturbances which were shaping his end, being used as instruments of divinity, were unrecognized by him. He was not a political preacher, and he was rods, chains and miles away from the notion of trying to work up new laws. The only time in his life he ever gave any advice to a ruler was in 1653, when he started as a lay preacher, and signed an address (with a lot of other folks) directed to Parliament regarding some local conditions in Bedford. They say he was rather a solid citizen at this time, and making a little money, and therefore his name meant something on the paper.

As far as Bunyan was concerned he put no faith in princes. Charles the Second when he was a refugee over in Holland (still popular with royal runaways) published the Declaration of Breda, which among other things had promised "liberty of conscience to all in religious matters as long as their views did not disturb the peace of the realm." But Bunyan knew better. To Bunyan this world was only a necessary evil, and folks were living in it just for one purpose—to get right with God, and so live that they would get to heaven. You cannot read his books without finding that out. So, right then, what kings and Parliaments promised, or did not, worried him very little. In a way all of this was going to affect Bunyan, affect him most profoundly. But the laws which kings made, God would judge them for. He would pray that Caesar might be righteous, but if he were not righteous he would still pray for him.

At this time Bunyan's greatest concern was his own character. A study of his life reveals that he was trying to fulfill all the law's demands. He was a Christian, and yet some passages of Scripture were troubling him. He knew that the man who kept the law ninety-nine per cent, and yet failed in one point, was guilty of the whole. While he was a Christian he was not entirely free, and he was trying to add cubits to his spir-

itual stature by taking thought. In spite of all
this he was doing some writing at this time. He
had published two small pamphlets: one against
extreme Quaker mysticism; and now, in 1658, he
published a sermon, based on the parable of the
rich man and Lazarus, with the significant title,
"A Few Sighs from Hell, or the Groans of a
Damned Soul, and etc., by that poor and contemptible servant of Jesus Christ, John Bunyan."

The active exercise of preaching will do a
great deal for a man spiritually, and it will help
settle his mind. If he is the right kind of a man
and is desperately in earnest he can help to convert himself. It has been done; but a man has to
be honest clean through to do it. And, with the
help of the Lord, he can preach assurance into
his own soul. Probably something like this happened in the case of Bunyan, for we see in
"Grace Abounding" that God sent the Holy
Spirit to be a witness with his spirit that he was
a child of God and had passed from death unto
life; so when the order came for his arrest, in the
fall of 1660, he was down to bedrock in his soul
quest.

Do not get the notion that John Bunyan
went around with a chip on his shoulder, and

courted arrest. He was not trying to be a martyr, although he was the stuff out of which martyrs are made. As far as he was concerned he paid little attention to unjust law. He was called to preach the gospel, and as with St. Paul, it was a case of "Woe is me if I preach not the gospel." Also, true disciple that he was, he would say with Peter and John, "It is better to obey God than man." Of course he would have preferred that he be left alone and allowed to preach; but if there was a notion that a man-made law could keep him from preaching,—well, it was so much the worse for the notion. The only people who had any effect on him were his own brethren, and he consented when they asked him to preach what they called a farewell sermon on the night he was arrested.

Bunyan Arrested

This last meeting was to be in a cottage in Lower Samsell. The people came from everywhere in the neighborhood to the farmhouse which was in the middle of a meadow surrounded by large trees. It was just like the Apostolic Christians once again meeting in the house of a

member. It is said that Bunyan got there a little
early, and did what many a preacher does today:
walked around the house out in the air, waiting
for the people to get there. Some of the people,
knowing the intense bitterness of the local
authorities, thought that possibly he had better
not preach; he was too valuable to be locked up.
Like Paul, when the elders wept over him, he
recognized the truth of what they were saying,
and yet he refused to be turned back. He knew
that if the shepherd was smitten the flock would
flee; but he knew also that if the shepherd proved
to be a coward they would all commit spiritual
suicide. He had the spirit of that great man who
did so much for him, Martin Luther, who, when
advised not to go into Worms for fear of Duke
George, said he would go into Worms if it rained
Duke Georges for several days handrunning; so
Bunyan likewise was not going to be turned back
by a miniature Duke George in the person of an
officious local justice.

The meeting had just begun. Bunyan,
after the prayer, had begun to preach to the people when the village constable and a local deputy
came in, and, ordering Bunyan to stop, told him
to come along quietly. Bunyan told the people

not to worry about him, as they were suffering persecution for righteousness sake, which was a whole lot better than being arrested for some real crime. The constable must have been of the type that believes that even a short sermon is too long. He grabbed Bunyan and hustled him off.

Bunyan was led before the local justice, named Francis Wingate, of Harlington House. In studying the history of the Wingates I cannot get out of my head the term, "codfish aristocracy." They belong to that to-be-pitied class of folk who believe that culture is like a coat of varnish; something that can be applied thick with a brush from the outside. They were not lords of the manor; they had few acres, but on one occasion Charles the Second had paid them a visit. They preserved the blue china this royal non-such ate on; in spirit, they encased it in a shrine and burned blue punk before it. Bunyan knew this Wingate, and knew that the Wingates had an ancient grudge long a-hungered and waiting to feed fat on the Dissenters. They were Royalists to the core; Wingate's father had fought in the Royalist army, but the son was taken for safety to the King's Quarters at Oxford by his mother.

Noncombatants are usually more bitter than combatants—especially after a war, and Wingate was just dying to do something mean. When Bunyan came before him for trial he was greatly disappointed to find that the folks gathered for the meeting were not armed. He opened amenities by asking Bunyan why he did not mind his own business, meaning, of course, that his business was mending old pots. Bunyan told him that he could do that in the daytime and preach at night. Wingate got peeved at this, and told him that he would "break the neck of these meetings." Bunyan was unruffled, and said very mildly, but we have no doubt with a gentle undercurrent of sarcasm, "Maybe"—which was about as good an answer as I think could be made.

He Could Have
Saved Himself

Bunyan was bound over to the Sessions, three months hence, and while the justice went into another room to write out the order committing Bunyan to jail, the vicar of Harlington came in to have some fun with Bunyan. He started in to abuse Bunyan, but the prisoner was the calmest man in the lot. He pointedly told this officious outsider that he did not have any business with him right then; that he was there to see the justice. The vicar wanted to know if he could prove that he had a right to preach. Bunyan countered very neatly by saying that he had Scripture for it, quoting from the first Epistle of St. Peter, "As every man hath received the gift even so let him minister the same." The vicar came back with a feeble attempt at sarcasm, asking Bunyan if he had heard of Alexander, a coppersmith, who disturbed Paul. Bunyan knew that his being a tinker was the cause of that remark. The vicar's Countercheck Quarrelsome was neatly turned by Bunyan's Retort Courteous when he asked the vicar if he recalled something in the gospels to the effect that the Scribes and Pharisees had their hands in the blood of the Lord Jesus. Just then a verse of Scripture flashed into Bunyan's mind: "Answer not a fool according to his folly." I have no doubt the vicar was intensely relieved —I would have been if I had crossed swords with John Bunyan and the Lord had whispered to him to be quiet and let me down easy.

Drawn by Ralph Chessé

BUNYAN IN PRISON

Mr. Froude, who has written in some ways a splendid criticism on Bunyan, as far as scholarship is concerned, makes light of his arrest, and at times seems put out with Bunyan for going to prison when he could have kept out by merely promising not to preach. But Mr. Froude never had a call to preach as St. Paul had, or Martin Luther, or John Bunyan. He had no great spiritual experience in his life. Sin had never swept like a sirocco over his soul, and he knew more of Piccadilly Circus and the pleasant quarters of Mayfair than he knew of the City of Destruction. He was a cultured and scholarly gentleman, a brilliant essayist, but no man can know John Bunyan unless he understands the spirit of John Bunyan, unless he has had in some measure the experience of John Bunyan.

John Bunyan was not a reed shaken by the wind, not a man who wore soft raiment or dwelt in king's houses hobnobbing with royalty. The people of his time doubtless did not understand John the Baptist, rough and straightforward and terribly in earnest; and to Mr. Froude, Bunyan is a voice crying in the wilderness where nobody can hear it, and where it will do no good. There is a tradition, and it may not be more than that,

that John the Baptist could have saved his head
if he had but consented to the caresses of Salome.
Bunyan could have saved his life and lost it right
at this critical moment. They even told him what
to say; all he would have to do would be to
indulge in a mental reservation and a little secret
evasion of mind; but he refused to do it.

It was probably November 13th, 1660, and
Bunyan was at that time 32 years of age. The
exact date of his birth is not known, but he was,
as you know, baptized on November 30th, 1628,
and he may have celebrated his birthday by going
to jail. He was sentenced to what they call the
Bedford county jail, to there wait for the January Quarter Sessions. And so in January, 1661,
Bunyan was haled before the county magistrates,
five of them, sitting "en banc." All of them were
unanimous in their opinion that Noncomformists
in general and Bunyan in particular were poison.
A certain Sir John Kelynge (Bunyan called him
"Kellin") who afterwards became Lord Chief
Justice, noted for his lack of law knowledge and
his want of judicial temperament, presided. He
had a record of browbeating witnesses and juries.

I do not suppose that we have any notion
today of some of those so-called courts of justice

in the seventeenth century. A writer of that time,
not a Noncomformist, said that the courts were
then little better than "caverns of murderers." A
picture of these courts where justice was "dis-
pensed with" can be found in Hallam's Constitu-
tional History of England, and the worst picture
of all is what followed later in the time of James,
when the unspeakable Jefferys and the Bloody
Assizes came upon the scene. Jefferys became
high in the favor of the king, becoming Lord
Chancellor, his portfolio punctuating with a
bloody period a long sentence of crime against
the helpless. In that day some judges browbeat
prisoners, took their guilt for granted, insulted
and silenced witnesses for their defense, and even
cast juries into prison under penalties of heavy
fine for venturing to bring in verdicts contrary
to their wishes. It was nothing at all for a judge
to give the miserable miscreant on trial before
him "a lick with the rough side of his tongue,"
preparatory to roaring out with lurid abuse and
curses the sentence of torture or death. Court
procedure has gone forward a few parasangs
from that pitiful and perfervid period.

The indictment against John Bunyan,
laborer, was that he had "devilishly and perti-

naciously abstained from coming to church to
hear divine service, and was a common upholder
of unlawful meetings and conventicles to the
great disturbance and distraction of the good sub-
jects of this kingdom, contrary to the laws of our
Sovereign Lord, the King." Justice Kelynge
acted as prosecuting attorney as well as judge. He
asked Bunyan why he did not go to church, and
Bunyan replied that he did go; he went to the
Church of God, where he was a member and
where Christ was the Head. This seemed to his
judgeship worse than useless, and he wanted to
know why Bunyan did not come to the parish
church. Bunyan and the judge got to arguing
about the Prayer-book. It was Bunyan's opinion then, whether he expressed it at that time or
not (as he did afterwards), that those who had
the spirit of prayer.prayed without the book and
were to be found in jail; while those who had the
form of prayer and could not do without the book
were found in the ale-houses.

Tried and Imprisoned

One of the justices, seeing that his colleague
was getting the worst of it in the argument,

wanted to stop Bunyan, but Justice Kelynge told him not to worry, as the Prayer-book was in no danger, "having been ever since the Apostles' time." They asked Bunyan if Beelzebub was not his god; others said he was possessed of the devil. Bunyan began to quote Scripture, using it to interpret his belief, just as he did later in Pilgrim's Progress, but they did not want any of that. They called it, "peddler's French," and "canting." Then the presiding justice though inveighing against preaching, turned preacher himself, and said "As every man hath received the gift," that is, as every man had received a trade, "so let him follow it." He intimated that Bunyan's trade was mending old pots, not meddling with souls. Bunyan showed the justice that this was eisegesis, not exegesis, and that he ought to get the context, which referred to the oracles of God.

The judge cut the matter short in anger, by asking Bunyan if he confessed to the indictment. He did not; but he was, nevertheless, remanded back to prison for three months. If at the end of that time he would not agree to go to church and quit preaching he was to be banished from England. If, after that banishment he was found in the country, without the royal privilege, he was to be hanged. As Bunyan was leaving for prison he turned to the justices and said quietly, "If I were out of prison today I would preach the gospel again tomorrow, by the help of God!"

Bunyan preserved this scene in the amber of his intellect, and put a touch of humor in it to relieve its grimness when he described that court scene in Vanity Fair in the Pilgrim. We give you just a taste of it. One of the witnesses against Faithful, Mr. Pickthank, is speaking. We reproduce it in all of its terse and graphic wit.

"When this Pickthank had told his tale the judge directed his speech to the prisoner at the bar, saying, 'Thou runagate, heretic and traitor, hast thou heard what these honest gentlemen have witnessed against thee?'

"Faithful. 'May I speak a few words in my own defense?'

"Judge. 'Sirrah, sirrah, thou deservest to live no longer but to be slain immediately upon the place; yet that all men may see our gentleness toward thee let us hear what thou hast to say.' "

As Bunyan expressed it, on being delivered to the jailor's hands, "I had home to prison again." Things were breaking bad for the Dissenters at this time. Some Fifth Monarchy men who aimed at the subversion of all earthly governments, arguing that it was only a short time anyhow until the Fifth Monarchy be set up, broke loose in London under a leader named Thomas Venner, and started a riot. They were arrested, and the English government took it as a good excuse to put the screws literally and figuratively to the Dissenters. This made it harder on Bunyan in prison, but he put the situation in a nutshell when he showed that it was no argument against his preaching at a peaceable gathering. "Thieves might come out of the wood, but all men coming out of the wood are not thieves." Several well-meaning folks went to Bunyan in jail and argued with him. They told him he was in danger of being transported, and possibly worse than that might happen. They urged him to do the little that was required of him—just drop into church once on Sunday, and if he must preach why preach to individuals.

But sham never got very far with John Bunyan. He hated it with all his soul, and you can see that with every turn of the road in the Pilgrim. You remember Formalist and Hypocrisy, and Mr. Legality, Mr. Facing-both-ways,

Mr. Anything, and a good many others. Bunyan said to one of these Job's comforters, "Sir, the law hath provided two ways of obeying: the one to do that which I in my conscience do believe that I am bound to do actively; and where I cannot obey actively then I am willing to lie down and suffer what they shall do unto me."

Let no one believe that Bunyan liked being in jail; no man in his senses would. Again the very highly cultured Mr. Froude argues that the life of a man in jail in England at that time was not such an unhappy one, and that jail life was almost like living at home. I am beginning to believe that Mr. Froude never even saw the inside of an English jail. Even today they are different from American jails in that they have none of the earmarks of our better country clubs. A century after Bunyan lay in Bedford jail John Howard, the great prison reformer, who, by the way, was later a member of the Bunyan church in Bedford, found a whole lot of things in English prisons which would not be permitted in a first class hotel.

The jail at Bedford was crowded with Dissenters, and they say that the "menage" was limited as to funds in caring for the guests. The average jail was allowed about twenty-five dollars a year to provide bedding, so they bought straw, and thus did they invest in rest. There was another drawback about going to jail then: the only thing they provided was room; board was not included; you had to feed yourself, and this looks to me a little like adding insult to injury. They say that even some of the homes in England at that time were so overrun with vermin that people would have to move out for a season to let the vermin die of starvation, and allow the house to "sweeten." Typhus was common in jails, and so was the cholera.

The Mettle of the Man

Besides all this Bunyan had a wife and four children dependent on him. His first wife had died two years before, and his four children were by this wife, all of them young and helpless. The oldest was a girl, born blind, whom Bunyan loved as the very apple of his eye. His second wife he had married a little over a year before, and she was with child when he was arrested. The news of his arrest was such a shock to her that she miscarried, and for nearly three weeks was at the point of death. More than that, to add to his anxiety, Bunyan expected to be hanged, and yet he could only bury his face in his hands and say with the tears streaming down his face, "I must, I must." To show you the mettle of the man (and this is worth preserving forever) we quote his own words when he was sent to prison:

"I saw what was coming, and had two considerations especially in my heart—how to be able to endure should my imprisonment be long and tedious, and how to be able to encounter death should that be my portion. I was made to see that if I would suffer rightly I must pass sentence of death upon everything that can properly be called a thing of this life, even to reckon myself, my wife, my children, my health, my enjoyments, all as dead to me, and myself as dead to them.

"Yet I was a man compassed with infirmities. The parting from my wife and poor children hath often been to me in this place (the prison in which he was writing) as the pulling of my flesh from my bones; and that not only because I am too, too fond of those great mercies, but also because I should have often brought to my mind the hardships, miseries and wants my poor family was like to meet with should I be taken from them, especially my poor, blind child, who lay nearer my heart than all I had besides. Poor child, thought I, what sorrow art thou like to have for thy portion in this world! Thou must be beaten, suffer hunger, cold, nakedness, and a thousand calamities, though I cannot now endure the wind should blow on thee.

"But yet, thought I, I must venture all with God, though it goeth to the quick to leave you. I was a man who was pulling down his house upon the head of his wife and children. Yet, thought I, I must do it—I must do it. I had this for consideration, that if I should now venture all for God, I engaged God to take care of all my concernments. Also, I had dread of the torments of hell, which I was sure they must partake of that for fear of the cross do shrink from their profession. I had this much upon my spirit, that my imprisonment might end in the gallows for aught I could tell.

"In the condition I now was in I was not fit to die, nor indeed did I think I could if I should be called to do it. I feared I might show a weak heart, and give occasion to the enemy. This lay with great trouble on me, for methought I was ashamed to die with a pale face and tottering knees for such a cause as this. The things of God were kept out of my sight. The tempter followed me with, 'But whither must you go when you die? What will become of you? What evidence have you for heaven and glory and an inheritance among them that are sanctified?'

"Thus was I tossed many weeks; but I felt it was for the Word and Way of God that I was in this condition. God might give me comfort or not as he pleased. I was bound, but he was free —yea, it was my duty to stand to his Word, whether he would ever look upon me or no, or save me at the last. Wherefore, thought I, the point being thus, I am for going on and venturing my eternal state with Christ, whether I have comfort here or no. If God does not come in, thought I, I will leap off the ladder even blindfold into eternity, sink or swim, come heaven, come hell. Now was my heart full of comfort." When it comes to devoted consecration, match John Bunyan if you can.

This second wife of John Bunyan, Elizabeth, was the type of a woman on which you could build a great nation. I am pretty strongly of the opinion that it would not hurt this country

at all to have a great many Elizabeth Bunyans.
She was a young woman, but you can see right
away that she had in her the stuff that ought to
cause the people of England to preserve her
memory forever with a statue in enduring bronze
right next to the man she loved so much. Consider this: she loved her step-children! Her devotion to these children and to her husband was
beautiful. She never sought for a moment to
have her husband compromise or stultify himself,
or do violence to his conscience. She was willing
to work her fingers to the bone to feed his children, and she did everything in her power to have
him released without compromising him.

A Woman as Brave and Dauntless as Her Husband

Let no one believe for a moment that this
fine, young, but poor woman, beautiful in face
and in spirit, though unlettered in books, was
anybody's fool or could not hold her own, even
when arguing with the Lord Chief Justice himself. A little while after Bunyan was arrested
the Midsummer Assize was held in Bedford.
Judges Twisdon and Chester and Sir Matthew

Drawn by Ralph Chessé

Elizabeth Bunyan
at the Prison Gate

Hale, the Lord Chief Justice, came. Bunyan wanted to get a new hearing in open court, and his wife tried three times to get the judges to consent.

Twice she presented the case to Sir Matthew alone, and once to all the judges. Her argument with these judges shows that she wielded a wonderful verbal rapier, fighting alone against three judges, although Sir Matthew Hale saw her side of the case, and at times tried to help her. On one occasion Hale asked her what was her husband's calling. You get a slant on the crowd in court who were listening in when the people called out, "A tinker, my lord." And consider her answer: "And because he is a tinker and a poor man therefore he is despised and cannot have justice" —which reminds us that it is still as hard for poor folks to get justice as it is to convict a million dollars.

During the course of the argument Elizabeth was so brilliant that Judges Chester and Twisdon got mad, and began to insult her. At the close of the argument Twisdon said that Bunyan's doctrine was of the devil. The reply of Elizabeth Bunyan was logical, and a queen could not have expressed herself better. She said, turn-

6

ing to Hale, who was the only one who seemed
to have any mercy in his heart, "My lord, when
the righteous Judge shall appear, it will be
known that his doctrine is not the doctrine of the
devil." Twisdon got mad at this, and urged Hale
to send her away, and Hale said something in
closing which bears on Bunyan's imprisonment,
showing the legal side of the case and also the
heart of the judge: "I am sorry, woman, that I
cannot do thee any good; thou must do one of
those three things aforesaid, namely: either to
apply thyself to the king, or sue out his pardon,
or get a writ of error; but a writ of error will be
the cheapest."

I am tempted to believe that this good
woman, as brave and as dauntless as her celebrated husband, furnished nine-tenths of the
moral support he received from any mortal while
he was in prison. She made it easier for him to
endure as seeing Him who is invisible.

Six Years in Prison

In the spring of 1662 Bunyan made strenu-
ous efforts to have his case brought before the
spring Assizes, but the local justices saw to it

that his name did not appear, and so he remained
in prison. Bunyan served six years in this first
imprisonment. He was honored by being the first
Dissenter to suffer for his faith. Minnows were
safe; the king and his henchmen at the beginning
were out after whales, and the biggest one in all
these troubled political and theological waters
was John Bunyan.

Bunyan helped to support his family by
making long tagged shoe laces, which were
peddled on the outside by hawkers. It is to be
presumed also that some of his friends helped his
family, although he says very pathetically in one
place, that the children were left to beg. In one
point the joke was on the government: Bunyan
was arrested for preaching in the open, but there
were at least sixty Dissenters in this little two-
story jail, and so Bunyan organized a church,
and preached in jail. The Dissenters living in the
town or in the regions roundabout, when they
wanted to worship with each other, would have
to sneak out in the woods at the dead of night,
preach in undertones, and hardly raise their voices
in song for fear of being heard by some "informer"; but here in the prison they could preach

and pray and sing to their hearts' content, and there was none to molest or make afraid.

There was one mitigation in the imprison-ment of John Bunyan, and that was the jailor, evidently a rare character for that time. Possibly he secretly sympathized with the Dissenters, and felt sorry for his prisoners; jailors often do, because they know what is going on, and they know some folks are in jail who ought to be on the outside. It is not hard to believe that a man who had even a little bit of fairness in his soul and a little of the milk of human kindness in his system could meet John Bunyan and not like him—not feel but that it was an outrage to have a man like him in jail, simply because he would not go to a certain church, and he wanted to preach. Even in that day, amid all the turmoil and prejudice and blindness, that sense of Brit-ish justice would occasionally come to the surface for air, as it did in the case of this jailer.

Every jail must have a few "trusties," and so John Bunyan was made a trusty, although the English did not call it that. In the first six years imprisonment, 1660 to 1666, Bunyan was often allowed to go home for a few hours and visit his family. In some cases he was even given leave to go to London. It is said that on one occasion he was given permission to stay over night, but he no sooner got home than he had an inward prompting to get back to the prison. Just as he got back and reported to the jailor a messenger came from one of the local justices asking if all the prisoners were in, and especially if John Bunyan was there. Some would call this a "hunch" or an intuition, but I am old-fashioned enough to believe that the steps of a good man are ordered of the Lord. John Bunyan lived so close to God that they could talk to each other, even in whispers.

The Plague Breaks Out
in London

Bunyan's first prison term ran the six years —1660, the year Charles the Second came to the throne, until 1666. He was in prison because he did not attend worship in the Established Church, and because he preached. Other severe laws were passed, and followed each other in quick succession, making it decidedly uncomfortable for the Dissenters. For instance, the Corporation Act made it obligatory on all holders of municipal offices to renounce the Covenant which the Puritans of England and Scotland had taken together, and compelled them to publicly take the sacrament of the Lord's Supper at a service of the Church of England. Then the so-called Act of Uniformity enforced the use of the Book of Common Prayer upon all clergymen and congregations; and as if this was not enough, the Conventicle Act, was passed, which forbade all religious assemblies whatever, except such as worshipped according to the Established Church. But so strong was that undercurrent of revolt throughout the country that something else was needed to "haud the wretches in order," and the Five Mile Act was passed, forbidding all Dissenting ministers from teaching in schools or settling within five miles from any incorporated town.

It is said that two thousand dissenting clergymen were driven out of their pulpits between sunup and sundown, and chased out of the towns they were living in by this last Act. The young and husky might work with pick and shovel for a living, but the older ones could beg. To resist one of these brutal, intolerant, senseless and unjust laws was punishable by heavy fines, imprisonment or deportation, which meant virtual slavery. Men were sent to the British colonies in the Indies to work in the swamps and die under the burning sun, simply because they could not pronounce "shibboleth." Some Dissenters were sent to Virginia as slaves, political slaves but freemen in heart and conscience, and they gave a transfusion of rich, red blood to this young country.

A strange catastrophe happened while Bunyan was serving this first six year term. In 1665 the plague broke out in London. Everyone who could even crawl out of the town got out. Parliament, the King, and his court and courtesans got out post-haste. Somehow they got the notion in their heads that they were worth saving, and they fled to Oxford, where Parliament and the king set up shop. Folks were dying in London like flies. It is said that a hundred thousand people died in six months. Mr. Pepys wrote in his diary on the 7th of June, 1665, that it was the hottest day he ever felt in his life. "This day, much against my will, I did in Drury Lane see two or three houses with a red cross upon the door, and 'Lord have mercy upon us' writ there, which was a sad sight." Among the brave men who remained in the stricken city were the despised Dissenters, who nursed the sick, consoled the dying, and with their own hands buried the dead, though courting death at every step of the road. As a reward for this they were persecuted harder than ever.

In 1666 the plague had hardly died out before a terrible fire visited London. Someone who saw it said that it "was not to be outdone until the final conflagration." The city of London, built of wood, was burned to the ground with the exception of a few houses in the northeast section. It is said that the advisors of Charles really delighted in the burning of the city, and saw in it an opportunity to crush without serious opposition the already harrassed Dissenters.

In Jail Again

This was the temper of the times when Bunyan was released in 1666. He was out of prison one day, and did what he said he would do—preached the next day. As soon as the local authorities could get the goods on him they set the legal machinery in motion, and in a few weeks he was back for his second imprisonment, which lasted another six years, until 1672. He was at liberty from '72 to '75, when he was again imprisoned, but only for six months. He did a world of writing in his first imprisonment, not so much in his second, and wrote his greatest book, the Pilgrim's Progress, in the third imprisonment. I will tell you all about it in the next section.

The Tinker
and His Thoughts

I know the popular conception is that John Bunyan put his hand on his brow one day, and said to himself, "Go to, now, we will produce a great book," and then wrote Pilgrim's Progress. Hardly. While I believe that the Pilgrim's Progress had as large a measure of inspiration as any book ever written, I know that Bunyan learned how to write by writing through the years. He tried his prentice-hand on more than two score books before he took his pen in hand to give the world this most delightful allegory.

John Bunyan was a writing man, and although he had learned nothing in the school of Aristotle or Plato; had never taken English IV, nor the "elements of poetics"; and could not spell for green apples, as we shall see later, he took to writing just as naturally as Lindbergh gravitated toward a business where he could defy the laws of gravitation.

While I do not recommend it, the jail was where John Bunyan learned to write. He did not spend all of his time in writing, to be sure, but after he got through working on shoe strings he took the curse off his imprisonment by reading and writing. His library consisted of the Bible and Fox's Book of Martyrs. It is said that the latter was in three volumes, folio, with Bunyan's name written large on the separate title pages. He did something that was common in that day, and wrote comments on the side of the text.

Someone said that Bunyan must have had a concordance in jail because of his numerous exact quotations from the Bible; but Bunyan swallowed the Bible in more ways than one, and, like the man in the Apocalypse who ate the book, it became very sweet in his system. He knew the Bible from cover to cover, and the Word was not only hid in his heart but ingrained in the cells of his brain and pulsing in his finger tips. Like John Ruskin, who was brought up on the Bible, it gave him a wonderful writing style. There is something in the Book which makes a man, after a while, put down his ideas in ink.

When "The Heavenly Footman" was printed in 1698, ten years after Bunyan's death, the printer published as an appendix a chronological list of Bunyan's works. This shows that

Bunyan began writing in 1656. His first was not a very large work (about a good sized pamphlet) and it has, as was the custom in that day, a very topheavy title. It was labeled, "Some Gospel Truths opened according to the Scriptures, or the Divine and Human Nature of Jesus Christ; His coming into the World; His Righteousness, Death, Resurrection, Ascension, Intercession, and Second Coming to Judgment, plainly demonstrated and proved; and also Answers to Several Questions, with profitable Directions to stand fast in the Doctrine and the Son of Mary against those blusterous Storms of the Devil's Temptations, which at this day, like so many Scorpions break loose from the Bottomless Pit, to bite and torment those that have not tasted the Virtue of Jesus, by the Revelation of the Spirit of God. Published for the good of God's Chosen Ones, by that Unworthy Servant of Christ, John Bunyan of Bedford, by the Grace of God Preacher of the Gospel of His Dear Son; Job. 14:6. Acts 4:12." At the beginning of his writing life he produced more than a dozen titles and as topheavy as this one.

In 1657 some Quakers came to Bedford, preaching their doctrine to the people. Bunyan heard them and was terribly stirred up. Especially did he take offense at the preaching of Edward Burroughs, the chief Quaker preacher, whom he calls in the title of the pamphlet he wrote against Quakerism, "a professed Quaker, (but proved an enemy to the truth)."

His Head in the Clouds but His Feet on Solid Ground

Like all great saints there was a good deal of mysticism in Bunyan's makeup; but while his head was often in the clouds his feet were on solid ground. The ethereal mysticism of the Quakers was too much for him, and that little pamphlet has a message for these times. Jesus Christ is, according to Bunyan, true man as well as true God. He is the Son of Mary, and though being in the form of God and dwelling in heaven he thought it not a prize to be clutched at to remain equal with God, but took upon himself the form of man, became incarnate in the flesh, born of the Virgin Mary, though conceived by the Holy Ghost. He grew as a flesh and blood boy, became hungry and tired, had nowhere to lay his head, endured the contradiction of sinners, was crucified, dying on the cross for the sins of the world. And we are saved by his blood and by his death in an atonement no one else could make. We are not simply saved by his teaching, but by his sacrifice on the cross; and this is no mere phantom, mystical Christ, but a Christ who was also in the form of his brethren in the flesh.

In 1658, while Bunyan was preaching and yet torn with doubts, he published a remarkable pamphlet called, "Sighs from Hell; or the Groans of a Damned Soul." He based his story on the sixteenth chapter of Luke—the story of Dives and Lazarus. Bunyan in his preface says that he writes it to "fitly serve as a warning word to sinners, both old and young, by faith in Jesus Christ to avoid the same place of Torment; with a discovery of the usefulness of the Scriptures as our safe Conduct for the avoiding the torments of Hell." A queer coincidence occurred at this time. As the pamphlet was published near the time of the death of Cromwell someone asked as to whether the advertisement of the book was a mere accident or the announcement of some Royalist trying to be funny. This was the first of his writings that ever got over a first edition.

When the list was printed in 1698 this work had run through nine printings.

You will note that Bunyan was writing a booklet a year. It was probably just before his arrest in 1660 that he wrote "The Doctrine of the Law and Grace Unfolded, or a Discourse Touching the Law and Grace." This is another long title running over a hundred words, and giving practically the contents of the thesis. He goes into the nature of law and grace, showing they are the two Covenants. And then for the help of the reader, in the back of the pamphlet there are questions and answers on law and grace. Of course it is really a sermon, and based on Hebrews 7:19; Romans 3:28; Romans 4:5. This was his longest work up to then; about 23 sheets in octavo, and on the title page there is this superscription, "Published by that Poor, Contemptible Preacher, John Bunyan of Bedford."

Centuries Ahead of His Times

In 1660 Bunyan was put in Bedford jail, and in 1661 the first book of his imprisonment appeared. It was titled, "Profitable Meditations Fitted to Man's Different Conditions, in a Con-

ference between Christ and a Sinner; in nine
Particulars. By John Bunyan, Servant of the
Lord Jesus." It is said that this book, published
in quarto, and (for the times) handsomely
printed, is now in the British Museum. It is in
poetical dialogue, and is supposed to be a conversation between Satan and a tempted soul.
Bunyan probably used some of this material in
the conflict between Christian and Apollyon.

His next book was in '63, "I Will Pray with
the Spirit and the Understanding also." It is a
discourse concerning prayer, and he divides it in
true preacher fashion thus: "What Prayer Is;
What it Is to Pray with the Spirit; What it Is to
Pray with the Spirit and the Understanding
Also." The same year he published "Christian
Behavior; a Map Shewing the Order and Causes
of Salvation and Damnation."

His next pamphlet was, "The Four Last
things: Death and Judgment, Heaven and
Hell." This was in verse. Two other small works
in verse followed: "Mount Ebel and Gerrizem;
or the Blessings and the Cursings," and "Prison
Meditations"—about a half sheet.

In 1665 his most pretentious book up to that
time, "The Holy City, or the New Jerusalem"

7

was printed. It is said that this book had its origin in a prison sermon. Bunyan, in the subtitle of the book, says he "will show wherein its goodly light, walls, gates, angels and the manner of their standing are expounded." He knows his limitations, and in the preface, which is addressed to "four sorts of readers," he opines that the learned readers will bite their thumbs at him because neither in line or margin has he a cloud of sentences from learned fathers.

The reference to writing in the margin, or "margent" as he expressed it, is interesting as it reveals a custom of the times. In the early editions of the Pilgrim's Progress Bunyan wrote some very interesting margins, proving that if he were living today he could get a job on a newspaper writing "heads." He naïvely states that he has neither the inclination nor the ability to write learned sentences. The "Holy City" treads on dangerous ground in that it is an exposition of the vision of the New Jerusalem given in Revelations, chapters 14-21. To him the New Jerusalem is not in the beyond; it is not the Church Triumphant so much as the Church Militant. He anticipated Blake's poem about bringing the New Jerusalem down to the green-commons of

England. This work is expressed in language typically Bunyanesque, reminding us of some of the quaintest passages of the Pilgrim's Progress. Note this: "Then will all the spiders and dragons and owls and foul spirits of Antichrist be brought to light, and all the pretty robins and little birds in the Lord's field most sweetly send forth their pleasant notes, and all the flowers and herbs of his garden spring."

In this book Bunyan shows a remarkable breadth of mind, being hundreds of years ahead of his time. No wonder all denominations are vying with each other in celebrating the tercentenary of his birth. Baptist though he was (and he has cast a luster on the name Baptist) he belongs to us all, as well as those noble Baptists who, throughout their history, have been pioneers in the fight for religious liberty. In the "Holy City" Bunyan goes on to say that on the foundations of the New Jerusalem are written the names of the twelve Apostles of the Lamb because it is their Doctrine that holds up the wall. The right preacher is the one who can preach this Doctrine of the Lamb as the Twelve preached it.

In England at that time the Prelatical hated the Papist, and they both hated the Quaker and the Independent; and the Presbyterians and the Anabaptists hated each other and all the rest of them, just as the others hated each other. In other words, among the various sects in England at that time there was a constant crossfire of hate, and a militant believer hit a head wherever he saw it. But Bunyan saw that not any one of them had a monopoly on salvation. He naively says that there is only one street in the Holy City, and that all the saints walk in one way and in one light. It is Antichrist that brought in all the crossings, by-lanes and odd nooks.

Here, as everywhere, Bunyan preaches the doctrine that salvation is a matter between the soul of man and God; and that it is what we are ourselves when we are alone with God that counts. Every man has to go through the River of Death alone, and it is the individual that will stand alone before the judgment bar of God, with no priest or preacher at his side to aid him to give an account for the deeds done in the body. He says that men must have pure hearts for that golden street; just as a clown with his dirty, clumping shoes is not admitted into the king's private chambers, so it is only golden men with golden hearts and golden shoes who shall be admitted into the Holy City.

Stone Walls and Iron Bars
Do Not a Prison Make

In the same year Bunyan published two other books: "The Resurrection of the Dead," discussing the question of the resurrection body, and adding a discourse on the last judgment and the end of the world. He wrote also a poetic work entitled, "Prison Meditations: Dedicated to the Heart of Suffering Saints and Reigning Sinners: by John Bunyan, in prison, 1665." Sometimes I question whether some folks ought to sing that hymn of Faber's, especially the second stanza, which goes,

"Our fathers, chained in prison dark,
  Were still in heart and conscience free:
How sweet would be their children's fate,
  If they, like them, could die for thee!"

I am merely saying what we all know and confess: it is a little strange to hear people who haven't enough iron in their religious blood to make a carpet tack, and who fall in a faint at the

very thought of death, singing about how sweet
it is to die for a conviction. But Bunyan in this
poetic work proves that stone walls and iron bars
do not a prison make. We get a flash of his mind
as he lay in Bedford jail in the following:

"For though men keep my outward man
        Within their bolts and bars,
    Yet, by the faith of Christ, I can
        Mount higher than the stars.

"Here dwells good conscience, also peace,
        Here be my garments white;
    Here, though in bonds, I have release
        From guilt, which else would bite.

"The Truth and I, were both here cast
        Together, and we do
    Lie arm in arm, and so hold fast
        Each other: this is true."

It is worth going to jail to be able to write a
poem like that, and to have such a spirit. Bunyan was superior to his surroundings. A good
many of us would have died of a broken heart to
be shut up for several years in a seventeenth
century English jail, but Bunyan had the same

comfort that St. Paul had when he was in the Mamertine prison, and got it from the same source, and should say, like Paul, and with a world of meaning, "I have learned in whatsoever state I am therewith to be content."

When Bunyan was just a little over five years in jail, in '66, he wrote one of his greatest books, "Grace Abounding to the Chief of Sinners." It is said that every man has a book in his system, and if he has lived with any adventure at all he can just dive down into his subconsciousness, grab up in his two hands the acts of his life, and come up with a book. Bunyan did this when he was five and a quarter years in prison, "waiting to see what God will suffer these men to do with me." In "Grace Abounding to the Chief of Sinners" he gave us a remarkable autobiography, more graphic than even Wesley's journal. He draws back the curtain and lets us see his whole life.

This is a book every lover of Bunyan ought to read. He tells of his boyhood, his wonderful find of Luther's "Galatians," and his love for his wife and children,—especially his blind child. He tells of his soul struggles, and, while admitting his swearing and Sabbath breaking, he defends himself stoutly from the vile calumny that was heaped upon him in latter life by those who were jealous of him. He reiterates that he was clean, as far as unchastity was concerned, from his youth up. As a spiritual autobiography competent critics rank it alongside of Augustine's Confessions. I regard Bunyan as better than the Bishop of Hippo in that he is a good deal more natural, simple and direct in his style.

Shortly after this book was written he was released from prison. How long he was out we do not know, but we know it was not very long. One of his contemporaries says, "A little after his release they took him again at a meeting, and put him in the same jail, where he lay six years more." Bunyan was just getting ready to preach. He says, "The subject I should have preached on even then when the constable came was: Dost thou believe on the Son of God?" Bunyan made good on his promise when first arrested, when he told the judges that if they released him one day he would preach the next. I wonder if we could not do today with a little of the constancy of John Bunyan? Here was a man who stood foursquare to all the winds that blew when he knew he was right.

During his second imprisonment possibly only one book was written; only one was printed, according to his biographers. There was a reason. Dr. Brown, his most voluminous biographer, who was in the line of succession as minister of the church at Bunyan Meeting, Bedford, for twenty years, says that at that time Bunyan's publisher could not get his books licensed. Evidently Bunyan's works, though non-political and highly spiritual, were anathema to the authorities, because they hated him and were afraid of his influence. His London publisher, Mr. Francis Smith, says that just before the great fire of London in '66, the censor of the press visited his printing office and carried off a good many of Bunyan's books.

King Charles in a Terrible Stew

Of course King Charles was in a terrible stew in those days. Within the royal palace his mistresses, if we may accept the word of Mr. Pepys and others, were giving him a good deal of trouble, and on the outside there was a great deal of discontent. It will be recalled that Holland established a colony on Manhattan Island at the mouth of the Hudson River, which was called New Amsterdam. England had a treaty with Holland, made by Cromwell, which recognized the Dutch claims in the New World. Two things possibly influenced Charles perfidiously to regard this treaty as a scrap of paper: one was his hatred for Cromwell, and the other was that Louis XIV wished to conquer Holland for the purpose of extending his own kingdom and forcing Romanism on the Netherlands.

By the secret Treaty of Dover the French ruler bribed the English king with a gift of 300,000 pounds to join forces with him against Holland. Charles never cheeped to Parliament on this little deal. There was another secret deal made: that Louis would pay Charles 200,000 pounds a year from the date when the English came and he should openly avow himself a Roman Catholic. Like the sneaking traitor he was, Charles sent a British fleet under the command of his brother, James, the Duke of York. They sailed under sealed orders, with the crew, and the nation, in total ignorance of their maneuver, and they finally came up the Hudson and demanded the Dutch Colony's immediate and unconditional surrender. The Dutch were not prepared to defend themselves, so the English took the town, and called it New York in honor of the royal brother who had perpetrated the robbery.

Shortly after the fire of London (Charles was at war with Holland at this time), the Dutch sailed up the Thames and took London. To give you an idea of England at that time it is said that Parliament had granted Charles large sums of money on different occasions to build and equip a navy, but that he had wasted this money on his mistresses. The English navy consisted of a lot of rotten hulks, with the sailors constantly behind in their pay, and always ready to mutiny. When the Dutch fleet sailed up the Thames there was no opposition. They burned the English boats, blockaded the river, and made Charles get down on his knees and beg for peace.

Charles at this time had intended to proclaim himself openly as a convert to the Church of Rome. He issued a proclamation of indulgence to all religions, with the hidden intention of favoring the Church of Rome especially. Bunyan was released from prison, and it must be recorded that once, and only once in his life, he was taken in by a man, for he went completely

wrong in his judgment of Charles. He believed
that Charles was acting in good faith, not knowing his secret meanness, and wrote an apprecia-
tive article along this line. He compared Charles
with the alien king who had been kind to the
Children of Israel. Of course Charles acted
without legal warrant in issuing this indulgence
without the sanction of Parliament. But that
was nothing new for Charles, for his sole ambi-
tion constantly was to rule without Parliament,
and extort from everyone all the money he could.

Parliament saw through his scheme, however, and what few Dissenters were in that body
fought the indulgence because it was illegal.
They knew also that Charles was working under
cover as to his real motive. So Parliament
passed a law requiring every government officer
to publicly acknowledge himself a Protestant.
Charles tried to conciliate them by marrying his
niece, Princess Mary, to William of Orange, the
president of the Dutch republic. This was a bad
move on Charles' part, for later William threw
James, Duke of York, off the throne.

Charles was a typical despot, and a poor sort
of man. A lot of men when they have trouble
in the business world take it out on their families

when they get home, while others, if they have any trouble at home take it out on the folks they work with. Whenever Charles had trouble with his mistresses, or with Parliament, he took it out on the Dissenters, and as it so happened John Bunyan was about the biggest individual sufferer. Right at this time Charles, chafing at his domestic and political reverses, began to tighten down on the Dissenters. This was the reason Bunyan went back to jail so quickly, why his books were confiscated by the censor, and his publisher given so much trouble.

We can understand now why the American colonists fought so strenuously for the freedom of the press, and why John Milton wrote that immortal document, "The Areopagitica" in which he flayed those in authority, drunk with power and blinded, who would kill a good book because it ran counter to their prejudices. No wonder our forefathers inscribed this freedom to print on their banners when they were fighting for liberty. How deep are the roots of English institutions embedded in our soil. There is something common between the two countries that nothing can destroy.

In Bunyan's second imprisonment he printed a "Defence of the Doctrine of Justification by Faith in Jesus Christ, showing through Gospel Holiness Flows from Thence." The title goes on further to say that Mr. Fowler's pretended design of Christianity proves to be nothing more than trampling under foot the blood of the Son of God, and idolizing man's own righteousness. This Mr. Edward Fowler had, early in 1671 while rector at Northill in Bedfordshire, published a book called, "The Design of Christianity." Mr. Fowler had been a Dissenter, was ejected in '62, and speedily conformed in order not to lose his "living." Like the immortal Bishop of Bray, it did not make any difference who was ruling or what the religion was; he was going to be Bishop of Bray if he had to change several times.

Bunyan Replies to Fowler

A copy of Fowler's pamphlet fell into Bunyan's hands while he was in jail, and he was fired immediately with the rector's heresies. Fowler was really a Unitarian, and, according to Bunyan, also a mixture of Quaker and Romanist. He

was preaching reformation rather than regeneration, and Bunyan says that he overthrew the
wholesome doctrine contained in the tenth,
eleventh and thirteenth of the Thirty-nine
Articles of the Church of England, while pre-
tending to be a minister in that church. There
were folks even in that day who did not know
what they believed, and some others who believed
everything and nothing. We see also the effect
of the universities on the pulpit, for Bunyan says
that Fowler did not get his doctrine from Scripture, but from the Cambridge thinker, John
Smith; "while John Smith goes in turn to Plato;
and so they wrap the business up."

Fowler argued also that in matters of worship we would have to leave it to whatever is
commended by custom or commanded by super-
iors. Bunyan reminded him that he hopped from
Presbyterianism to the prelatical mode, and if
there would be another change he would keep
going backward and forward. He wanted to
know what Fowler would do if he found himself
in Turkey. If Fowler was going to turn around
like a weathervane every time the wind shifted
simply for the sake of "sleeping in a whole skin"
Bunyan would just have to leave him to his fate;

but as far as he was concerned he was not influenced by man, but by God. It is thought that Bunyan was released from jail soon after he published his reply to Fowler. Thus ended his second imprisonment.

That Conventicle Act

In March, 1672, the Conventicle Act was superseded by the Declaration of Indulgence. This let Bunyan out of prison, and he returned to his Bedford home. Before we part with the Conventicle Act, and we are glad to part with it, there is one thing that must be said. It did more to corrupt the nation than possibly any Act of Parliament ever passed. To make this weak and unjust Conventicle Act grow teeth and claws a spy system was inaugurated, and an army of men and women were employed to act as spies and informers. The snooper you have with you always, and that was the age of the snooper, for it paid to be one. Men who could not make a living at anything else began to be able to wear good clothes through spying on folks.

You remember in Bunyan's story of "The Life and Death of Mr. Badman" there is a picture of English rural life of that time. Mr. Bad-man was the reprobate who professed religion until he married the good church girl, and "once aboard the lugger and the gal was his" he began to reveal himself. You will recall that he threatened to turn informer and report his wife for attending church. Bunyan said that Mr. Badman "had malice enough in his heart to turn informer," and he would have done it except he was a tradesman and was afraid he would lose all his trade if he did.

Bunyan cites the case of several informers who came to a bad end, which was just punishment for their snooping. However, snooping paid; some of them received as high as fifteen pounds for a successful conviction. The sons of Belial in every community quit working and turned informers. Of course the State was responsible, for it established a complete espionage system which ramified everywhere. There was a Spy-book found which was arranged alphabetically, which showed how the district around Bedford was under complete serveillance. It is significant to note that the spies reported that all over the country hundreds of people would gather at a time to attend meetings. Just before the death of the Act of Uniformity this spy system was at its worst, and seemed to be burning brightest, just as a candle flares up when in its shank it fries in its own fat.

Bunyan at Liberty

Bunyan was now at liberty for three years, and in that time did a great deal of writing. He published in '72 a "Confession of Faith and Reason of My Practice." In this booklet he discusses the question of open communion. He states in the preface that while he "dare not communicate with the open profane, yet I can with those invisible saints that differ about water baptism."

In 1873 he published another book traversing the same lines, entitled "Difference in Judgment about Water Baptism no Bar to Communion, or to Communicate with saints as saints proved lawful." This was an answer to a book written by the Baptists entitled, "Some Serious Reflections on that part of Mr. Bunyan's Confession of Faith touching Church Communion with Unbaptized Believers." In '74 he again wrote an answer to his critics within his own com-

munion, and titled it, "Peaceable Principles and
True, or a Brief Answer to Dr. Danver's and
Mr. Paul's books against my Confession of
Faith, and Differences in Judgment about
Water Baptism No Bar to Communion; wherein
their Scriptureless notions are overthrown, and
my Peaceable Principles still maintained."

These titles indicate that there was at that
time some healthy discussion in the Baptist
church, and that John Bunyan was a very broad-
minded man. He himself said, "I never cared to
meddle with unimportant points which were in
dispute among the saints; yet it pleased me much
to contend with great earnestness for the word
of faith and the remission of sins by the suffering and death of Jesus. I saw my work before
me did run in another channel, even to carrying
the awakening word; to that, therefore, I do
adhere." While he conceded water baptism to be
"God's ordinance," he refused to "make an idol
of it." He was like that character in the Old
Testament who said, "If thy heart is right in this
matter as my heart, give me thine hand." It is
said that Bunyan's arguments were so logical
and his leadership among the Baptists at Bedford so strong at this time that his church became

open communion, and fellowshipped those who believed in infant baptism.

Those Infamous Rumors

Do not imagine that John Bunyan was a hero, after this second imprisonment, to all the folks round about. He was a hero to most of his church folk, but as far as outsiders were concerned he fulfilled in his own person that saying of Jesus about a prophet not being without honor save in his own country. There were people on the outside who hated him bitterly, and they were only waiting for a chance to do him some meanness. They began to spread all kinds of infamous rumors about him. In the early part of 1674 a farmer lived at Edworth on the Bedfordshire border, named John Beaumont. He was a widower, and his unmarried daughter, Agnes, then 21, kept house for him. This farmer had sat under Bunyan's preaching, and wept with conviction. Folks are the same in all generations; John Beaumont had no depth of soil in his system, and when he left church and his neighbors laughed at him for listening to Bunyan he began to be ashamed and to feel mean toward Bunyan for making him a butt of ridicule in the neighborhood.

Agnes, however, seemed to have been a girl of strong convictions and independent mind, and she joined the Bedford Church at Gamlingay, Bunyan receiving her into the church. In February, 1674, she was anxious to be present at a meeting of the church there, and gained her father's reluctant consent. She was to go with a neighbor named John Wilson, who failed to come; and, as the roads were impassable on foot, and as Bunyan happened to ride up at the time, she asked to be allowed to ride with him on the pillion. Bunyan knew how her father hated him, and did not want to let her go, but she begged so hard that he finally consented. Her father saw them leaving, but could not plow through the mud to reach them. When Agnes came home that evening the door was locked against her. She spent that cold night in the barn, and next day went to her brother's house, where she stayed for a few days until her father came to his senses. She went home on Sunday, and the following Tuesday her father was seized with a fatal illness, and died suddenly.

There was a snooper in the neighborhood, who pretended to be a preacher, who was very jealous of Bunyan and he started a pretty bad story about Agnes, aided and abetted by a neighboring lawyer whom the girl had refused to marry. They said she had poisoned her father, and that Bunyan had helped her to do it. There was an official post-mortem examination conducted by the coroner, the charges were disproved, and there was every evidence that John Beaumont's death, while sudden, was natural. However, this proves how calumny would sear virtue itself.

That was not the only lie about Bunyan. They said he was a witch, because of his magnetic power in preaching and his ability to persuade people. They said he was a Jesuit in disguise and under the pay of the Pope; that he was a highwayman; that he had his misses, and two or three wives. He replied to these accusations in these words which are well worth being preserved, and show the nobility of character and the innate purity of the man: "My foes have missed the mark in this. I am not the man. If all the fornicators and adulterers in England were hanging by the neck, John Bunyan, the

object of their envy, would still be alive and well.
I know not whether there be such a thing as a
woman breathing under the cope of the whole
heavens, but by their apparel, their children or
common fame, except my wife."

Bunyan in Great Demand

Bunyan was a faithful pastor, and the
church records at Bedford show that there were
numerous church trials, but you may be sure that
the scandal-monger was given short shift. There
is a story of a lady, who, after being warned
privately not to peddle scandal, continued, and
was publicly rebuked. This woman was placed
on probation until she could reform and bring
forth fruits meet for repentence. There is a most
interesting entry in the church record at Bedford
administered toward a young lady who "had been
admonished for disobedience to her parents, to
wit, for calling her father liar, and for characters
to her mother."

During his pastorate at Bedford Bunyan
carried the Word to all the country round about.
He was in demand everywhere. Of course during this time there was more liberty than usual.

However, there were places where because of local conditions it was not well for meetings to be held except in secret. Here again John Bunyan encouraged his listeners and comforted their hearts by the Word of God.

Back Again to Prison

John Bunyan had liberty for three years, but in 1675 there were political changes. The king was anxious to grant a great deal of liberty to the Roman Catholics, and prepared an act called the Declaration of Indulgence, which suspended all the penal laws against the Romanists and the Protestant Dissenters. He ordered all the clergy to read this declaration from their pulpits on a given Sunday. The Archbishop of Canterbury with six other Bishops petitioned to be excused. The king refused to excuse them, and threw them in the Tower. One of the Bishops was Trelawney of Bristol, but a native of Cornwall. The news of his arrest roused the fighting spirit of those independent people, and all over the country, especially in Cornwall, the song spread like wildfire,

"And shall Trelawney die, and shall Trelawney
    die?
There's thirty thousand Cornishmen will know
    the reason why."
    And the miners took it up, and sang,
"And shall Trelawney die, and shall Trelawney
    die?
There's twenty thousand under ground will know
    the reason why."

In spite of the dire threats of James, the
jury refused to convict the Bishops, and, in spite
of all the pressure he could bring to bear, Parliament refused to pass his law. The result was
that Bunyan was again arrested and thrown into
prison for preaching, for the old laws were oper-
ative again, and with a good deal more vengeance.

The first and second imprisonments were in
the county jail, called by some Silver Street jail,
but the third imprisonment was in the jail over
the River Ouse, where Bunyan had been baptized
as a young man. It is admitted by practically all
critics that it was in this third imprisonment that
Bunyan wrote his Pilgrim's Progress. We have
shown that Bunyan was learning to write
throughout the years. When he went back for

his third imprisonment in '75 he had been writing since '56, a total of 19 years, and had written 22 books and pamphlets in that time. It is interesting to note that he lived sixty years and wrote sixty books.

The Seventeenth Century an Age of Writing

We stated that Bunyan was learning how to write, and he was doing it in the best school in the world. In this day we find ourselves reading so much that we haven't time to think. We spread out over so much territory that we become frightfully thin. Our stream of culture today is like Powder River up in Montana, which in places is a mile wide and an inch deep. Bunyan was drawing his inspiration from that font of Living Water, that well of purest English undefiled, the English Bible. You will remember that he had only two books in his library, Fox's Book of Martyrs, and the Bible. No wonder the Pilgrim seems inspired next to Holy Writ itself, and flashes and burns up with genius. Bunyan had all of the ruggedness and beauty and directness of the writers of the Bible, and in an age of excess book-baggage he demonstrated that a straight statement is the shortest way to make your point.

The seventeenth century was an age of prolixity. You remember the army of the Commonwealth and the army of the king carried printing presses around with them, and in the space of a few years England was smothered under pamphlets. The sainted Baxter, who was a chaplain in the Parliamentary army, and another Puritan divine, Dr. Owen, produced folio after folio like almanacs, writing seventy volumes each, most of them of formidable size.

They tell the story of a seventeenth century scribbler named Prynne, who wrote a library amounting to over two hundred books. He wrote a book against actors and acting. Henrietta Maria, the queen, wife of Charles the First, was, as you remember, a French woman, and she was also an amateur actress. When you couple that fact with the Gallic temperament you find someone who does not take to criticism kindly. This lady did not; she became offended at Mr. Prynne's book, and took it as a personal insult. Prynne was condemned to fine and imprisonment, was pilloried at Westminster and at

Cheapside, and had an ear cut off in each place. A contemporary who saw Prynne in the pillory at Cheapside informs us that while he stood there they secured all of his books they could in that place, and burned his large volumes under his nose, almost suffocating him, which was adding insult to injury.

However, they did not burn up all of Prynne's books—only those around Cheapside, so a rich but sentimental sister, who believed as Prynne did, bought up a complete edition, and put them in the library of a London college. When that school burned, these volumes were saved because being in folio they were considered the most valuable there. In other words, literature went by the ton in that day, and when you spoke of the weight of a book you meant avoirdupois. England was full of authors who had ruined booksellers, and it was an age in which it was said that it was easier to write up to a folio than to write down to an octavo; for correction, selection and rejection were either not known or looked down on.

Bunyan in Pilgrim's Progress shows the fine effect of the Bible on his style. He comes right to the point. Not only that, but as we have seen, most of Bunyan's other books were written for a purpose. He was either stirred up to controversy by a Quaker, an Established clergyman, an Antinomian, or his own brethren; or he wanted to correct some false doctrine in the world. But the Pilgrim's Progress was written for himself alone: he tells us that in the opening sentence. He wrote it because he could not help it. The figures came trooping out as soon as he set his pen to paper, and he could not put them back in the box any more than you can recall a word after you speak it. He never wasted time developing a character; the character was developed when it was born, and he, like a good artist, could draw a picture with a few deft strokes of his brush.

Bunyan's Writing Style—
"It came from my heart, so to my
head, and thence into my
fingers trickled"

Bunyan himself says that, "It came from my heart, so to my head, and thence into my fingers trickled." From his fingers he dribbled it daintily till he had it done. In the poetic preface he wrote to the Pilgrim, he repeats this thought, using a very homely figure of catching something by the tail and pulling it out of a hole, the size amazing you as you pull. This is what he said:

"Thus I set pen to paper with delight,
And quickly had my thoughts in black and white.
For having now my method by the end,
Still as I pull'd, it came; and so I penn'd
It down, until it came at last to be
The length and breadth and bigness which you
      see."

The Pilgrim was so good that it seemed too good to be true. That an untutored tinker could write it did not seem natural to the critics, so they accused Bunyan of plagiarism; but you will recall that in the end of the "Holy War" he goes on to say that the matter and manner was all his own, and nobody knew anything about it until he had finished it. He even resisted the temptation which besets the best of poets and authors in that he did not read it to anyone else while he was writing it. He repeats that no mortal knew of it until it was done, and that after that "by books, by wits, by tongues or hand, or pen add five words to it, or write half a line." All of it was his. We do not imagine that Bunyan himself even revised it, and we quite agree with Coleridge that to polish it would be to destroy it. Bunyan wanted it just as he wrote it, to chalk out before the eyes of the reader his Pilgrim, and to write it in such a "dialect" that all sorts and conditions of men might "get it."

When he was let out of jail he read the Pilgrim manuscript to some of the members of the Bedford church. The ultra-religious, especially those among them who lacked imagination or a sense of humor, threw several mental handsprings, and were shocked to death to think that their preacher would write anything so frivolous. Why, it approached fiction, and was almost in the form of a fairy story. He ought to be serious, forging thunderbolts, or directing a blast against the terrible army of sinners. He ought to be taking a fall out of the Antinomians and the Quakers, and he ought to be giving the Established Church some hard cracks for the way they had treated him. The whole thing ought to be done very seriously; no frivolity, mark you. Sancho Panza said on one occasion, "Bring your problem into council, and one will cry 'It is white' and the other 'It is black.'"

Bunyan found that out, and he found out that he would have to use his own judgment.

Fortunately a Few Said "Print It"

Fortunately there were a few of these good folks who had a little juice in their system, and they enjoyed it to the limit, and said, "Print it." Bunyan was fifty years of age at this time, and always did have a large reserve of good, hard sense, even recognizing his youthful spiritual conflicts; but you remember how he passed through much that would have driven another man crazy. He settled the whole matter by sensibly putting his emotions aside and deciding it on the Word of God. So he printed it.

We presume it is the custom today for some of the highly educated to bite their thumb at Bunyan's book, and to raise a supercilious eyebrow; but let them have their fun. When they produce a book which stands a chance of lasting two hundred and fifty years we will take them a little more seriously. You remember the story of John Marshall, Chief Justice of the United States, who, after hearing his pastor preach on the parables of Jesus, said that anybody could write a parable. "All right," said the preacher, "write me a few for next Sunday." "Very good," said Marshall, "will half a dozen do?" "Plenty, if you can get that many finished in that time." The preacher met Marshall the next Saturday. "How about my parables? Are you ready to deliver them?" Said the great Chief Justice, who could write an opinion on law as easily as most folks can write a letter, "I have been trying all week, and have not been able to write one."

Macaulay said there were a lot of bright men in England in the first part of the seventeenth century, but there were only two of them that had the imaginative faculty to a marked degree: one was John Milton, who could write in Latin as well as he could in English, and who gave the world Paradise Lost; the other was John Bunyan, who could not spell but who gave the world the Pilgrim's Progress.

Some folks thought that Bunyan copied from Spenser's Faerie Queen. This is enough to make you laugh. Spenser's Faerie Queen is about the most unreal thing ever written. It is said that it has one unpardonable fault, the fault of tedi-

9

ousness. People do not go far into it until they
become sick of cardinal virtues and deadly sins,
and they long for the society of plain men and
women. Macaulay said, "Of the persons who read
the first canto not one in ten reaches the end of
the first book, and not one in a hundred per-
severes to the end of the poem. If the last six
books, which are said to have been destroyed in
Ireland, had been preserved, we doubt whether
any heart less stout than that of a commentator
would have held out to the end."

Full of Live Folks

On the other hand, the Pilgrim's Progress
is the only allegory ever written which had all of
the earmarks of being alive. No wonder those
friends of Bunyan in Bedfordtown advised him
to print it. It was too good to be lost. They
knew all of the characters; most of them lived
right around the corner, and they rubbed elbows
with them at least six days out of the week, and
some of them seven. They knew Christian because they knew Bunyan. All that Bunyan had
to do to give us the character of Christian was to
look into his own heart. These people knew

Pliable—weak, easily persuaded Pliable, who believed what the last man he talked to told him, but was ready to run as soon as he got his feet wet at the Slough of Despond. They knew Obstinate, a typical beef-fed, bull-headed Englishman: there were dozens of this fellow in every town. And you did not have to go to the Lord of the Manor to find the character of well fed, over-dressed, over-stuffed Mr. Worldly Wiseman, who dwelt in the town of Carnal Policy, and who directed Christian to "a gentleman named Legality, who dwelt in the village of Morality." The early wood-cuts made Mr. Worldly Wiseman look as pompous as Henry the Eighth. They knew "a man whose name was Talkative," who had an innocent, open faced expression, and an ever open mouth, and who could talk all day and say nothing. They knew Hypocrisy, whose eyes were closed as if in prayer, his right hand extended as if delivering the apostolic benediction, and whose left hand was behind his back ready to take a bribe, and saying out of the corner of his mouth, "Slip it to me." They knew Ignorance, who knew nothing but was not aware of it, but who, with a face shining like a new tin pan, was always smirking

Drawn by Ralph Chessé

THE SLOUGH OF DESPOND

and smiling, and who, while he could not prove a thing, based his hope of eternal life on the supposition, "I am always full of good notions." These characters are not only alive, but they march, march—not the march of the wooden soldiers—not the march of marionettes; they march with the swing of those who were full of red blood corpuscles, whether they be good or whether they be bad.

Forced Upon the Critics by the Common People

It is because the book is full of live folks that it appealed to the people; the common people at first, for the literati were jealous, as usual, and resented a tinker poaching on their preserves. They believed, like the judges of Bedford, that Bunyan had better stick to pots and pans and leave souls and literature to his betters. It is one of the books that the common people forced on the critics, and the critics were forced to accept it because they could not help themselves.

Pilgrim's Progress has been the "vade mecum" of thouands of earnest Christians for two hundred and fifty years. Young and old, rich and poor, learned and unlearned, have rejoiced in it, and wept over its pages. It has been baptized with the tears of thousands of earnest hearts. Many a soul it has led to Christ. Thousands seeing Christian with the burden on his back decided to go on a pilgrimage with him, and felt the burden roll away when he led them to the foot of the cross.

There is no question of the work of genius in the Pilgrim's Progress. Taine, the great critic, says that Bunyan has the freedom, the tone, ease and clearness of Homer. The first edition of the Pilgrim reveals the fact that Bunyan was a natural writer, and not a product of the schools. Take his spelling, for instance. When it came to spelling Josh Billings could not hold a candle to him. We know that there was a good deal of off-side spelling in that day, but Bunyan never let the spelling book get in his way. For example, he spelled the word die in three ways: "die," "dye," and "dy"; he wrote for Slough of Despond, "Slow of Dispond"; "ay" for aye; "bien" for been; "bruit" for brute; and "rayment" and "rainment" for raiment; "strodled" for straddled.

It is said that there is nothing remarkable in doubling the final consonant in such words as "generall" and "untill," for that was the seventeenth century custom, but Bunyan doubles it in such words as "bogg," "denn," "ragg," "wagg," and, what is even more unusual, he doubles the medial in such words as, "hazzard," "fellon," "eccho," "widdow." He dropped his final e's, writing "knowledg," "bridg," but he uses the "e" to give the old plural form, making it "shooes," "braines," "alwaies." He was strong on colloquial expressions and grammatical irregularities, writing "catched up," "shewen," "ditest," "then for to go," "I should a been," "afraid on't," "such as thee and I," "you was."

Bunyan did not spell brains according to the dictionary, but he had them all the same, and all that is needed to produce a great book is brains. You can write your book with lead pencil on butcher's paper, spell like Josh Billings, and disregard punctuation marks, but if you have "braines" or "brains"—either form will do as long as you have them—a hard-boiled publisher will even send you a prepaid telegram accepting your book.

It is said that the printer corrected a good deal of the spelling in the first edition. I wonder if any writer is a genius to his proofreader? However, in the second edition there were fewer mistakes in spelling but more typographical mistakes. Bunyan wrote some striking subheads on the margins in the first edition which were evidently "killed" by the printer or proofreader in the second edition. For instance, "Ignorance jangles with them"; "How to carry it to a fool," and "Talkative talks but does not."

The first edition cost one shilling and six pence. The first editions of the Pilgrim were printed on something that resembled thin butcher's paper, and a man had to enjoy good eyesight to read it. Of course it was meant for tinkers, and farriers, house maids, carters, colliers and farmers. It never came out of the kitchen, and it never showed its snub nose in a drawing room for the good and simple reason that the folks who bought it had no drawing room, and were not permitted in the drawing room of the folks they worked for.

But the common people read it gladly, and it crept over the land as gently and as surely as a spring zephyr goes from the channel to the

Thames. After awhile some of the upper circles wanted to know what all the noise was about, and they demanded a de luxe edition. This was given them on white paper, and to make it "deluxer" still there were some fearfully and wonderfully made wood-cuts added. After awhile the critics read it, and while some coughed behind their hands, and others scoffed, the more sensible among them prayed for a like gift, offering to give all they possessed in exchange for it. Macaulay says that when that majestic old mentor, Dr. Samuel Johnson, who hated a Tory like everything, got the book, he broke over his usual rule of never reading a book through, read the Pilgrim from cover to cover, and then was peeved because there wasn't more.

The Second Part of Pilgrim's Progress

The second part of Pilgrim's Progress, "The Story of Christiana and Her Children," was published in 1684, six years after part one. It is a beautiful story, but does not compare with part one in the sustained interest and delineation of character. It seems to lack alignment in parts, and is not as kinetic as the story of Christian. Some of the critics think that Christiana in her beauty and strength represents Elizabeth Bunyan. However, Christiana's children were four sons, while Bunyan's were three sons and three daughters. But that is not a real difficulty. I am inclined to believe—possibly because I want to believe it—that Christiana is Elizabeth, his second wife, and Mercy is his first wife, Mary.

There are some artificialities in part two that never occur in part one. Take the character of Mr. Sagacity for instance. In the first part the characters are mostly men; in the second part they are the female counterparts of these men. It is distinctly feminine. There is Mrs. Lightmind, Mrs. Know-nothing and Mrs. Bat's-eyes. In the House of the Interpreter there is Muckraker (you will recall President Roosevelt's reference to it, which reminds us of Bunyan's influence even in this day). You remember Mercy and the man who courted her. There is some humor in this courtship, but yet it seems rather out of place on a pilgrimage such as they were on.

In this second part, however, is one of the finest little poems Bunyan ever wrote. Bunyan wrote a good deal of poetry, some of it good, and some of it not so good; but to my mind one of the prettiest pieces of verse he wrote is the Song of the Shepherd Boy, which Mr. Great-heart, that beautiful character, calls attention to:

"He who is down need fear no fall,
　　He that is low no pride:
He that is humble ever shall
　　Have God to be his guide.

I am content with what I have,
　　Little be it or much;
And, Lord, contentment still I crave,
　　Because Thou savest such."

Bunyan's "Holy War" Is Published

In 1682 Bunyan was at liberty, and had more leisure to write. The Pilgrim, published in '78, was probably bringing him in some money, and his financial condition being improved he could devote more time to writing. In '82 he published "The Holy War made by Shaddai upon Diabolus for the Regaining of the Metropolis of the World; or the losing and taking again of the Town of Mansoul." In the Pilgrim the soul of Christian and his companions is the thing of great concern; the "Holy War" deals with the souls of the race; it is the struggle between Shaddai and Diabolus—God and the Devil, over the souls of a community.

Bunyan was an intense individualist. He believed that the only remedy for the redemption of the world was the regeneration of the individual; but in the "Holy War" he recognized that individuals run cities; the regenerated man runs the city for God, while the unregenerate runs it for the devil. A regenerated individual can do a lot of good as an individual, but his power for good is increased when authority is placed in his hands; the opposite holds true with a sinner. One sinner destroys much good, and his power for destruction increases as authority is placed in his hands.

You will recall that when James the Second was on the throne, during the intense period of Bunyan's persecution, Bunyan addressed a letter to the king, showing his loyalty. This bears on the Holy War, for Bunyan recognizes that the acts of the ruler have long arms and reach down into the ordinary affairs of the citizen. He says, "I believe that by magistrates and powers we shall be delivered and kept from Antichrist. Let the king have verily a place in your hearts, and with heart and mouth give thanks to him; he is a better savior of us than we may be aware of." Of course Bunyan puts his personal religious experience into the story of the many individuals who take part in the Holy War. While the city as a whole has to be redeemed, Bunyan is sure that Diabolus must not have the slightest corner in it. This is his short poem in the preface:

"Then lend thine ears to what I do relate
Touching the town of Mansoul and her state;
How she was lost, took captive, made a slave,
And how against him set that should her save,
Yea, how by hostile ways she did oppose
Her Lord, and with his enemy did close,
For they are true; and he will them deny
Must needs the best of records vilify.

"For my part, I myself was in the town
Both when 'twas set up and when pulled down.
I saw Diabolus in his possession,
And Mansoul also under his oppression:
Yea, I was there when she him owned for Lord,
And to him did submit with one accord.

"When Mansoul trampled upon things divine
And wallowed in filth as doth a swine,
When she betook herself unto his arms,
Fought her Emmanuel, despised his charms;
Then was I there, and did rejoice to see
Diabolus and Mansoul so agree.

"Let no man count me then a fable-maker,
Nor make my name or credit a partaker
Of their decision. That is here in view
Of mine own knowledge I dare say is true."

Typical Bunyanesque Passages
in The "Holy War"

The Holy War is a story of salvation. It deals with man's first disobedience in the Garden of Eden in eating the forbidden fruit; with the fall of man from his high estate of purity; with the coming of the law which would redeem those who had revolted; and finally, with the coming of the Son in redemption; and while man is redeemed, still he is a free agent, and while saved is not safe. This in brief is the story of the redemption of Mansoul, whose maker and builder was Shaddai, in the country of Universe.

While the subject is more ponderous than the Pilgrim and the movement is slower, comparable only to the moving of old-time engines of war as compared to lithe Pilgrim, still there are some typical Bunyanesque passages which no one but this "tinker out of Bedford" would have thought of. For instance, no aliens were allowed to enter the city, and the walls could not be broken down from the outside; the only breach possible was from the folks on the inside. The city has five gates: Ear Gate, Eye Gate, Mouth, Nose and Feel Gate; in other words, the five senses. Diabolus, who had been a servant of Shaddai, but who had rather reign in hell than be a servant in heaven, is now the king of the blacks, or negroes, representing the fallen angels. He consults with Beelzebub and Lucifer, and takes Lucifer's advice to try to crawl in as a snake. Thus we see the Eden story.

He comes to the wall, asks for a parley, and tells the good folks in the town—Captain Resistence, Lord Will-be-will, Mr. Conscience, the Recorder, and Lord Understanding, the Lord Mayor, that he is an interested neighbor who has observed their slavery, and wants them to be free. There is a tree growing in their garden that has fruit that will make them wise. The people, believing Diabolus, run to the apple tree; Ear and Eye Gate are opened, Diabolus enters, becomes the king of Mansoul, and establishes himself in the castle, which is the heart of man. All of the vile followers of Diabolus take the public offices: Lord Lusting is made Lord Mayor, and there is a new Board of Aldermen: Mr. Haughty, Mr. Swearing, Mr. No-truth, Mr. Drunkenness, Mr. Cheating. We still have some of them as aldermen in some American cities. Of course Bunyan saw the town of Bedford "new modeled," and he used it here.

Now with Mansoul in the hands of the unregenerate, something must be done by the forces of righteousness, and so the army of Shaddai appears before the town of Mansoul with war engines to break down the walls. This is the law and the Old Testament dispensation. But as before, it is only the people inside who can effect a breach. Bunyan's short experience in the Parliamentary army, where they marched and countermarched, attacked and were attacked, and threw their strength against cities or defended them, came in valuable here. Finally the Son, Emmanuel, comes, and calls on the town to surrender. Diabolus makes all sorts of offers to compromise; to give up half of the town, finally just to reserve a room in the castle where he can have his relatives and friends visit him for old time's sake, but all offers are rejected; he must not have an inch of room.

The town is assaulted and won, and Emmanuel comes in dressed in golden armor. The people come as penitents, their leader with a rope around his neck. They are sure they are going to be executed, and they say they ought to be; but their sorrow is deep and their contrition is real, and, to their amazement, they are freely pardoned by the Son who loves them. All of the bells ring with joy, and the people are so happy they do not sleep that night. Mansoul is again in the hands of the good and true.

They now have two teachers to instruct them: the Spirit of Truth, the Holy Spirit, and Mr. Conscience. There is a new city government of godly men. However, there are some enemies still within the wall: Carnal Security, and Mr. Present-good. Bunyan was like John Wesley in that he believed that wealth was the great corrupter, even of good people; and Bunyan draws a picture of human nature with one eye on the

10

earth and the other on heaven. The big danger now is that as goodness has brought prosperity they will make the castle, the heart, a warehouse overcrowded with goods, instead of a place where warriors for the truth will abide. "The cares of this world, and the deceitfulness of riches"—that is always the danger.

Then there is another danger: an army of Blood-men, who are reinforced by an army of Doubters, twenty-five thousand strong. They send in a summons to surrender, but are captured by the forces of Emmanuel. The traders within the gates are slain with one exception, Mr. Unbelief, "A nimble-Jack" they could never get hold of, who escapes—and is still abroad. That is another stroke that is as true as life. After this execution the King calls his people into the square, and encourages them to continue in his life until his coming again. There is rather an indefinite ending, and Bunyan had to leave it that way because the fight is never over until a man is out of the world.

While the Holy War cannot be compared to the Pilgrim, yet we feel that Macaulay had some grounds for saying that if the Pilgrim had not been written the Holy War would be the best allegory in the English language. There are places where the Holy War is unnatural, ponderous and far-fetched, and yet it has a great deal to redeem it: interesting characters, bright lines, vivid action, and a theme as large as all creation. Besides that, it shows that Bunyan knew that the heart of the natural man was deceitful above all things, and desperately wicked, and there was not a move of the enemy of souls that he did not know because of his early conflicts with Satan.

Bunyan Knew What He Was Doing

Bunyan not only knew the heart of an individual by experience, but he knew what a machine of oppression an aggregation of individuals could construct. He knew that men could organize themselves under what they called society, and conduct a warfare against their brother-men which would be diabolical. It was because Bunyan had this information of wholesome organized wickedness down so pat that Rudyard Kipling wrote, during the World War, this remarkable poem:

"A tinker out of Bedford,
    A vagrant oft in quod,
A private under Fairfax,
    A minister of God;
Two hundred years and thirty
    Ere Armageddon came
His single hand portrayed it,
    And Bunyan was his name.

"All enemy divisions,
    Recruits of every class,
And highly screened positions
    For flame or poison-gas;
The craft that we call modern,
    The crimes that we call new,
John Bunyan had 'em typed and filed
    In Sixteen Eighty-two.

"He mapped for those who followed,
    The world in which we are—
This famous town of 'Mansoul'
    That makes the Holy War.
Her true and traitor people
    The gates along her wall,
From Eye Gate into Feel Gate,
    John Bunyan showed them all."

After Pilgrim's Progress appeared Bunyan's name was up, and prosperity began to come to him. This was the same year as the Popish Plot excitement, and when the names of Whig and Tory first appeared in political history. There was a lot of bitterness still in the land, and yet there was a lot of opposition to the king and his measures, so Bunyan was unmolested. Besides, he was now a popular idol, not only of the Baptists but of all the Dissenters. When he went out on preaching engagements it was like some exceedingly high dignitary making a visit. So complete was his rule over the Baptist Church that he was called, "Bishop Bunyan."

A Great Preacher as Well as Writer

Bunyan was a great preacher as well as writer. This was natural. He had in the first years of conviction deep, startling, extraordinary convictions. From the time he was ten years of age he began to think on religious things. He had a remarkable experience of conversion. He knew the Bible from cover to cover, and he worked out his own system of systematic theology. He confined himself to the Bible and one or two other books, and he had plenty of time to concentrate, being most of his natural life in jail.

Wherever he went to preach in his later years crowds thronged his ministry. When he came to London a thousand people would get out to church at seven o'clock in the morning to hear him preach, and three thousand people would come in the afternoon, hot or cold, rain or snow, and many would be turned away. He had the magnetism and the power of the orator, but above all he preached in the demonstration of the Spirit and of power. One of the king's chaplains, a serious-minded man, went to hear him preach, and the king twitted him for wasting his time going to hear a tinker. He replied, "Your majesty, if you will pardon my saying it, I would exchange all of my learning and everything else I have for that man's gift."

Bunyan always had a vital message; he preached with a purpose. In "Grace Abounding" he says: "In my preaching I have really been in pain, and have, as it were, travailed to bring forth Children to God; neither could I be satisfied unless some fruits did appear in my work. If I were fruitless it mattered not who

commended me; but if I were fruitful I cared
not who did condemn. I have thought of that,
He that winneth souls is wise; and again, Lo,
children are an Heritage of the Lord; and the
fruit of the Womb is his reward. As arrows in
the hand of a mighty man, so are Children of the
Youth. Happy is the man that hath filled his
Quiver full of them; they shall not be ashamed,
but they shall speak with the Enemies in the
Gate.

"Sometimes, again, when I have been
preaching, I have been violently assaulted with
thoughts of blasphemy, and strongly tempted to
speak the words with my mouth before the Congregation. I have also at some times, even when
I have begun to speak the Word with much
clearness, evidence and liberty of speech, yet
been before the ending of that Opportunity so
blinded, and so estranged from the things I have
been speaking, and have also been so straitened
in my speech as to utterance before the people,
that I have been as if I had not known or remembered what I have been about, or as if my head
had been in a bag all the time of the Exercise.

"Again, when at sometimes I have been
about to preach upon some smart and searching

portion of the Word, I have found the Tempter suggest, What! will you preach this? this condemns yourself; of this your own Soul is guilty. Wherefore preach not of it at all; or if you do, yet so mince it as to make way for your own escape; lest instead of awakening others, you lay that guilt upon your own Soul, as you will never get from under. But, I thank the Lord, I have been kept from consenting to these so horrid suggestions, and have rather, as Sampson, bowed myself with all my might to condemn Sin and Transgression wherever I found it; yea, though therein also I did bring guilt upon my own Conscience! Let me die, thought I, with the Philistines, rather than deal corruptly with the Blessed Word of God. Thou that teachest another, teachest thou not thyself?"

His last sermon was in a church at Whitechapel on Sunday, August 19, 1688, from John 1:13, "Who were born not of blood nor of the will of the flesh nor of the will of man, but of God." His concluding exhortation was "Be ye holy in all manner of conversation." What he said deserves to be quoted and remembered: "Consider that the Holy God is your Father, and let this oblige you to live like the children of God, that ye may look your Father in the face with comfort another day."

An Errand of Mercy
Leads Bunyan to His Death

His death was characteristic of him. He was looked upon by all the Baptists as an arbiter, and was often called to settle disputes. In August, 1688, he went from Bedford to Reading to reconcile a father and son who were estranged. He was successful in bringing them together in peace and harmony. Going from Reading to London on horseback he was caught in a pouring-down rain. He reached the home of a friend, John Strudwick, on Snow Hill, London. Strudwick was a grocer, a member of a London Baptist Church, and a great admirer of Bunyan. Bunyan was thirty-six years older than Strudwick, but they were congenial friends. It must have been about the middle of August that Bunyan entered Strudwick's house, for on the nineteenth he preached at Whitechapel.

At the same time he was sending his last book through the press, "The Acceptable Sacrifice," based on the seventeenth verse of the fifty-first Psalm, "The sacrifices are a broken spirit; a broken and a contrite heart, O God, thou wilt not despise." Like all serious-minded and dynamic men, Bunyan felt that he ought to work even when he was sick. Perhaps if he had gone to bed and stayed there when he got to Strudwick's house around the eighteenth he would have lived longer; but it is hard to keep an energetic man in bed.

Many of the sayings of Bunyan during his last illness have been preserved. You will remember that when Christian and Hopeful are going over the river on the other side of which is the City of God, that it is written after Christian had feared, "Christian, therefore, presently found ground to stand upon, and so it followed that the rest of the river was but shallow. Thus they got over. Now upon the bank of the river on the other side they saw the two shining men again, who were waiting for them; wherefore being come out of the river they saluted them saying, 'We are ministering Spirits sent forth to minister for those that shall be heirs of salvation.' Thus they went along toward the gate."

And so Bunyan, crossing over the river "found ground to stand upon." His religion was very real to him, and heaven was sure. There was no more fear in his heart. His dying words were, "Weep not for me but for yourselves: I go to the Father of our Lord Jesus Christ, who will, no doubt, through the mediation of his Blessed Son, receive me, though a sinner, where I hope that we ere long shall meet to sing the new song and remain for everlastingly happy, world without end."

On Friday, August 31, 1688, John Bunyan died. When the news reached the church at Bedford the place became a Bochin, a place of weeping. He was carried to Bunhill Fields, Finsbury, which Southey called "the Campo Santo of the Dissenters." Like his Lord, he lay in the tomb of a friend, for John Strudwick purchased a new tomb for his honored guest. It is remarkable that while since Bunyan's time a lot of people who have started what they call a new religion have grown wealthy, Bunyan with all his genius was not able to leave much for his family. He regarded not riches. His faithful wife, Elizabeth, was left the sum of 42 pounds and 19 shillings. This was all she had except the royalties on his books, which were not very great because the books were sold not so much for profit as to do good.

Bunyan had six children: four by his first wife, Mary, and these were, Mary, the blind girl, Elizabeth, John and Thomas; by his second wife, Elizabeth, he had a girl named Sarah, and a boy, Joseph. Mary, his blind child, died before him. Like other great geniuses his children did not inherit his genius, and his first-born son, John, became a tinker and carried on business in Bedford till he died in 1728, one hundred years after the birth of his father. The other children married good, but ordinary men, and the family has just about disappeared.

Bunyan's Own Portrait

You will remember that when Christian goes into the House of the Interpreter there is a picture on the wall, and this is what he sees of the man in the picture: "He had eyes lifted up to heaven, the best of books was in his hand, the law of truth was written upon his lips, and the world was behind his back." How true that was of John Bunyan, for he drew his own picture there. He had but one destination, and that was heaven;

one book, and that was the Bible, the book which made him; nothing but grace and truth flowed from his lips, and the world was ever behind his back. You remember in Vanity Fair that the pilgrims viewed with disdain, and had no mind to buy the merchandise of the fair, such as "houses, lands, trades, places, honors, preferment, titles, countries, kingdoms, lusts, pleasures and delights of all sorts."

Bunyan felt the spirit of the message that Paul wrote to the Church at Corinth when advising them that the time was very short; that those who had wives should live as if they had none; buyers should live as if they had no hold on their goods, and those who mix in the world live as if they were not engrossed in it, for the present phase of things is passing away. Bunyan was absolutely unselfish, and was never spotted with this world. When he got up in the world he found that folks were always wanting to do something for him. When he needed their help he could not get it; but when he did not need it, and could look out for himself, his books were bringing him in a little money. "To him that hath shall be given," is the way it always works. In later life a London merchant offered to take his

Drawn by Ralph Chessé

Giant Despair

son into his house. He replied, "God did not send me to advance my family, but to preach the gospel."

On one occasion a friend complimented him after the service on the "sweet sermon" he had delivered. He said, "You need not remind me of that; the devil told me of it before I was out of the pulpit." It was said he never spoke of himself, never bragged of his talent, but seemed low in his own eyes. He never reproached nor reviled anyone, not even those who put him in prison. He had mighty fine judgment in his last years, and he made it his study not to give offense.

Like Moses, who in his youth had been a fire-eater and killed a man, Bunyan, though a high-strung youth, became one of the meekest men who ever lived. A friend who knew him and drew a pen-picture of him said he was "tall of stature, strong boned though not corpulent, somewhat of a ruddy face with sparkling eyes, wearing his hair on his upper lip; his hair reddish, but in the latter days sprinkled with gray; his nose well set, but not declining nor bending; his mouth moderate large, his forehead somewhat high, and his habit always plain and modest."

The first copy of Pilgrim's Progress could be bought for a shilling and sixpence; the same book today would command thousands of dollars. The warrant for his arrest in 1672 recently sold for over $1,500. More people know of John Bunyan today than did when he was carried to Bunhill Fields. His body is there, but his book has gone to every quarter of the world.

Secrets of Success

What were the secrets of Bunyan's success? Every biographer has pointed out that his style was made by the Bible. This is true. In the seventeenth century men did not only read the Bible but they believed it and spoke it literally. They expressed themselves in biblical terms. That purest well of English undefiled, the Bible, was the version that came from the order of King James. It was young then, having been on the market only a few years, and its poetry and sound and stalwart English did more to influence English speech than any other book. The Puritan went to the Bible to get his figures of speech, and when he would describe a thing it would be most often in the language of the Scriptures.

You remember how Cromwell compared wicked kings to Agag and wicked queens to Jezebel. When he described a battle, for instance the Battle of Dunbar, which was his "crowning glory" and the "clowning glory" of his adversaries, the sun was rising and he gave the order to attack, and it was in the language of Scripture that he encouraged his troops, and afterwards described the event. "Let God arise, and let His enemies be scattered. Like as the sun riseth, so shalt thou drive them away."

The Scripture swallowed up conceptions of Government. You will remember that Cromwell was offered a crown three times, and he would have liked to take it, too, but why didn't he? For the good and simple reason that the Scriptures in the minds of the Puritans were against it. They wanted no king but Jehovah; they were willing to have a President or a Protector, but the idea of the theocracy was so strong in their minds that the only king that they prayed for was the King of Kings who would establish his kingdom on earth. You remember the Fifth Monarchy Men and the desire to set up the reign of King

Jesus. That is just how far the Bible dominated the age.

Bunyan said he was never out of the Bible either by reading or meditation. He did not have to bring in his biblical illustrations by the ears. The truth is it was hard for him to describe anything without having recourse to something in the Book. When we discuss Bunyan's style we can see at a glance that the Bible shaped it.

However, there is one factor in his style which is the very essence of simplicity which is overlooked. He says in his preface to "Grace Abounding" that his experience with God was the mainspring of his simplicity. His words are well worth quoting: "I could have enlarged much in this my Discourse of my Temptations and Troubles for Sin; as also of the merciful Kindness and Working of God with my Soul. I could also have stepped into a Style much higher than this in which I have here Discoursed, and could have adorned all things more than here I have seemed to do; but I dare not. God did not play in convincing of me; the Devil did not play in tempting of me; neither did I play when I sunk as into a bottomless pit, when the pangs of hell caught hold upon me: wherefore I may not play in my relating of them, but be plain and simple, and lay down the thing as it was. He that liketh it, let him receive it; and he that does not, let him produce a better." We are quite in agreement with Bunyan. It would be hard for us to believe, however, that the Lord ever influenced anybody to be voluminous. We agree to the inspiration of simplicity—but not prolixity.

He Stocked the Fodder Low

Of course Bunyan had the good sense to stock the fodder low, putting it within reach of the common people, and a book which the common people can get, the critics are sure to understand by and by. It took the critics a hundred years in Bunyan's case, for even Addison was turning up his nose at Pilgrim's Progress; but the critics finally knuckled under. Bunyan never got above his raising, and never tried to. If he did not wield the sharp, polished Damascus blade of Saladin, he did wield the heavy and effective English battle-ax of Richard the Lion Hearted; and he could, with one stroke "cleave a churl to the chine." One swing of his verbal poleax and you dropped in your tracks.

Get down the Pilgrim and select any page you want, and see how it abounds in short, unadorned but strong Anglo-Saxon words. He used these with greater effect than any man who put a pen to paper, and I do not even except Chaucer. Pure Anglo-Saxon lends itself to alliteration, and Bunyan had this poetic quality. Notice it in the proverbs he left, such as, "A bird in the hand is worth two in the bush"; "Penny wise and pound foolish"; "Hedges have eyes and little pitchers have ears." He was intensely colloquial, but every natural writer is.

I have read a great deal on Bunyan, but I have never found a single reference to his prayer life; most writers hardly refer to it, and yet it is the biggest thing in his life, along with his intense study of the Bible. You cannot understand him without taking his agonizing with God in prayer into the equation. If it had not been for his habit of earnest prayer he would have slipped his eccentric.

You will remember in "Grace Abounding" he tells of reading some "Ranter's" books, and meeting some of these wild brethren. He said he had one religious intimate companion, a poor man, who "turned a most devilish Ranter," and gave himself over to uncleanness. The Ranters were the Holy Rollers of that day, and a good many of them had the notion that if they had ever been converted they could do anything and it would not make any difference; once saved always saved. They condemned Bunyan as legal and dark, saying that when a man had attained perfection he could do anything he wanted and not sin. These doctrines were pleasing to the flesh.

Even in His Prayer Life
Bunyan Retained His Humanity

Bunyan was then but a very young man, and, as he says, "my nature in its prime." They wrote mighty plausible things in the books about attaining to spiritual perfection, and spiritual perfection was what he wanted. But what did he do? His common sense and his spiritual urge made him go to God in prayer, and his prayer is characteristic, showing that he had that wonderful faculty of being able to understand himself. Note it: "O Lord, I am a fool and not able to know the Truth from Error. Lord, leave me not to my own Blindness, either to approve of or condemn this Doctrine. If it be of God let me not despise it; if it be of the Devil let me not embrace it. Lord, I lay my soul in this matter only at Thy feet; let me not be deceived, I humbly beseech Thee." After he was delivered from this delusion he blessed God who had put it into his heart to pray, for he said he had seen the effect of that prayer in preserving him, not only from Ranting errors, but those which sprung up afterwards.

His habit of prayer saved him in later life also from some grevious mistakes. When he was having his controversy with his own brethren regarding baptism and communion he might have become intolerant if he had not prayed; prayer kept him humble and sane. He could never pray the prayer of the Pharisee, even when honors were being heaped on him, "O Lord, I thank Thee I am not as other men are," but, like Luther, who thanked the Lord that he had made him a poor, simple man, so Bunyan retained his humanity. That was an age when the theological world was broken into as many pieces as a glass snake, and every contentious sectary was dead sure that he was right, and dead sure, too, that the other fellow was wrong. But Bunyan refused to

leave the right track. He said, "I would be as I
hope I am, a Christian. But for these factious
titles of Anabaptist, Independent, Presbyterian,
and the like, I conclude that they come neither
from Jerusalem nor from Antioch, but from
Hell or from Babylon." This is a sentiment that
some folks ought to be reminded of today. Bunyan was more than three hundred years ahead
of his time.

There was no spiritual pride in Bunyan,
either. Although he had a wonderful experience
he never bragged about it. A sense of our infirmities will keep a man from being a Pharisee
and a fool. You will recall that in the "Holy
War," though the people in Mansoul were delivered, still they were subject to certain temptations. This is the experience of all Christian people, and it was Bunyan's experience. He said:
"I find to this day seven Abominations in my
Heart: 1. Inclinings to Unbelief. 2. Suddenly
to forget the Love and Mercy that Christ mani-
festeth. 3. A leaning to the Works of the Law.
4. Wanderings and coldness in Prayer. 5. To
forget to watch for that I pray for. 6. Apt to
murmur because I have no more, and yet ready
to abuse what I have. 7. I can do none of those

things which God commands me, but my corruptions will thrust in themselves. When I would do good evil is present with me.

"These things I continually see and feel, and am afflicted and oppressed with; yet the Wisdom of God doth order them to my good. 1. They make me abhor myself. 2. They keep me from trusting my heart. 3. They convince me of the Insufficiency of all inherent Righteousness. 4. They show me the necessity of fleeing to Jesus. 5. They press me to pray unto God. 6. They show me the need I have to watch and be sober. 7. And provoke me to look to God, through Christ, to help me and carry me through this world."

That Saving Grace of Humor

Bunyan had a sense of humor. You can see that all through his writings. The Pilgrim's Progress has been called the "great epic of Puritanism." It represents the Puritan mind more than anything Milton ever wrote. But Bunyan though a Puritan of the Puritans in conduct had a sense of humor which like a bubbling well came to the surface, rippling and

sparkling. You get touches of it everywhere.
For instance, in the Pilgrim, Formalist and
Hypocrisy do not enter by the Strait Gate, but
come tumbling over the walls; and they tell
Christian that in their land of Vainglory the gate
was too far around, so they always took a short-
cut. Take the character of the judge who tries
Christian and Faithful at Vanity Fair; after
abusing Faithful for all he is worth he tells him
that he is going to show him how good and gentle
he can be.

Take the character of Talkative, who could
set his tongue to work and then go off and leave
it, and come back and find it hitting on all six.
He could talk on anything at a moment's notice:
heavenly things, earthly, moral, evangelical,
sacred, profane, things past or to come; things
foreign or things at home; things essential or
things circumstantial. This Talkative—the son
of one Say-well, dwells in Prating Row. Christian has to smile at him, for he says, "This man
is for any company and for any talk; as he talk-
eth now with you so will he talk when he is on
the Ale-bench; and the more drink he hath in his
crown the more of these things he hath in his
mouth; religion hath no place in his heart, or

12

house, or conversation; all he hath lieth in his tongue, and his religion is to make a noise therewith."

Another sample of Bunyan's humor is found in the character of Mr. Byends of the town of Fair-speech. He brags about his well-to-do relatives, Lord Turn-about, Lord Time-server, Lord Fair-speech, "from whose ancestors that town first took its name"; there is also Mr. Smoothman, Mr. Facing-both-ways, Mr. Anything, "and the parson of our parish, Mr. Two-Tongues, was my mother's own brother by father's side; and to tell you the truth I am become a gentleman of good quality; yet my great grandfather was but a waterman, looking one way and rowing another." This Mr. Byends married Lady Feigning's daughter. This considerate couple never strove against wind and tide; were always most zealous when religion went in silver slippers. But read the book for yourself, and chuckle over the quaint humor.

In 1701 a London Puritan published some poems that Bunyan had written, which he entitled, "Country Rhimes for Children." A good many of these poems were full of delicious humor, but the publisher, who had no funnybone, threw out twenty-five of the seventy-four "rhimes" on the ground that they were too humorous, and he gave this book for children the sobering title of, "Divine Emblems." You will recall in the preface to the Pilgrim that Bunyan asks, "Would'st thou in a moment laugh and weep?" He knew that there was humor in the book, and he left it there.

Bunyan the Poet

Bunyan had the poetic gift highly developed. We are quite sure he knew nothing about spondees, pentameters and hexameters; he cared nothing for literature as literature. Whether he wrote prose or poetry he was always aiming at one thing, and that was to help the souls of men. He knew nothing about measuring verse; in fact he was unhampered by any artificialities whatever. We do not mean that he was a great poet, for some of his poetry was like Mephibosheth in that it was lame in both feet; but some of it was the real stuff. There is no straining after effect; everything is natural, and there is a homely beauty about it. He saw it in the sunrise, in the clouds and in the trees. Read these lines:

"Look how brave Sol doth peep up from beneath,
Shows us his golden face, doth on us breathe;
Yea, he doth compass us around with glories
Whilst he ascends up to his highest stories,
While he his banner over us displays,
And gives us light to see our works and ways.
And thus it is when Jesus shows his face,
And doth assure us of his love and grace."

And read this more serious poem:

"Sin is the living worm, the lasting fire;
Hell soon would lose its heat could sin expire.
Better sinless in hell than to be where
Heaven is, and to be found a sinner there.
One sinless with infernals might do well,
But sin would make of heaven a very hell.
Look to thyself then, keep it out of door,
Lest it get in and never leave thee more."

They Copied Him, Satired Him — Tried to Improve Upon Him

They say that imitation is the sincerest flattery. If those in heaven are capable of being flattered we can picture Bunyan leaning over the golden bars and feeling a delightful glow. It was his prayer that his book should have free course like the Word of God to run and be glorified. It was his desire that men should treasure it up and profit by it, but he never expected some things to happen. For instance, only five years after Bunyan's death a conscienceless literary pirate named J. Blare, whose address was the "Looking-glass on London Bridge," felt that he could get somewhere on Bunyan's name, so he printed part three, saying that after the two former dreams of Christian and Christiana, his wife, he fell asleep again and had another dream, and he was generously giving it, for a price, of course, to an expectant public. He signed it "J. B.," which could mean either John Bunyan, or J. Blare. During his lifetime Bunyan had hinted at a third part, and of course everybody who had read parts one and two wanted this third part, so it sold very readily.

A great many imitations followed. One was entitled, "From Methodism to Christianity." This was around 1680. The politicians took it up, and there was one called "The Statesman's Progress, or a Pilgrimage to Greatness." Brown says, that this was directed at Sir Robert Wal-

pole, who was called Badman, who went to
Greatness Hall to get the Golden Pippins, which
he used as bribes to corrupt Parliament. There
was a political Pilgrim's Progress in which a Pilgrim sets out from the City of Plunder, and the
burden on his back is our ever-discussed subject
of "Taxes." One of the most amusing was a
book entitled, "The Pilgrim's Progress of John
Bunyan, for the use of children in the English
Church," written by an Established clergyman,
a Warden of Sackville College, Oxford. As a
piece of brazen effrontery it is hard to beat, and
yet it is really funny.

Bunyan was pretty broad minded, as we
have shown, but if he had a pet abhorrence it was
the use of the Prayer-book and the ceremonies of
the Established Church. During his pastorate at
Bedford a certain Robert Nelson quit going to
the meeting-house and began to attend the
Established Church, being received into that
communion by confirmation. Bunyan was horri-
fied; he and his members threw Robert Nelson
out of the church on the grounds that "he was
openly and profanely bishopt after the Anti-
christian order of that generation; to ye great
profanation of God's order and heartbreaking of

his Christian brethren." Now this pious church
warden went to work and made baptism as a
means of spiritual life, placing a well in the garden at the Wicket Gate, into which Christian
dips himself three times "the which when he had
done he was changed into another man," and at
the baptismal well his burden rolled away. The
House Beautiful becomes the Ceremony of Confirmation—you remember what Bunyan said
about "profanely bishopt." The writer of this
remarkable summersault says in justification that
this is the way Bunyan would have written it if
he had known better.

And then Nathaniel Hawthorne, years
afterwards, taking a shot at the flabbiness of
religious life in his day wrote a satire. He goes
to the City of Destruction, and finds that a
Pilgrim does not have to walk any more: there
is a railroad from that place to the Celestial
City; the Slough of Despond has been all sur-
faced over, and you go through the Hill Difficulty by the way of a tunnel. The silver mine
of Demas is paying dividends, and Doubting
Castle is a fine, modern building with all the
conveniences. There is a steam ferryboat going
to the Celestial City. The only drawback is that

no one knew whether it ever reached the other side or not. There were whole flocks of pilgrims twittering in long primer for young and old, for men and women, for preachers and politicians; there were burlesque Pilgrims, and some wag got after the pious church warden and had Bunyan's ghost go on a pilgrimage to the bedroom of this good brother, and scare him half to death.

Another interesting event occurred when a good vicar in 1811 published what he called a "corrected edition" in which he said he "improved the phraseology of the author, elucidated his obscurities, and did away with his redundancies." This edition illustrated that to attempt to improve on Bunyan was to ruin him. Of course it went out of print with his first edition, while Bunyan's work is still going on. John Wesley published an amended edition in 1774.

The Universality of Pilgrim's Progress

The great beauty of the Progress is that all churches can unite on the book. The picture he draws of his Pilgrim is not a sectarian one but a Christian one. Possibly every missionary society under the shining heavens, whether it be Congregational, Baptist, Presbyterian, Episcopal, have all ordered the book published for their work in the foreign field. It appeals to the native simplicity of the people they are working with. Even the Roman Catholics have printed the book as is, except the reference to Giant Pope.

In Japan they have Christian in a kimona, working his way up the Hill Difficulty; in China the House Beautiful is a pagoda; in Arabia he wears a white burnous, and the keepers of the vineyard, who read the book while they watch the grapes, feel that Christian is one of them and that he fits into their country quite as naturally as a palm around an oasis. It is the universal book with characters which have that touch of nature which makes the whole world kin.

In the peat bogs of Ireland and where the River Shannon flows they read in the evening light the story of the Pilgrim. It is read by the fiords of Norway, in the chill of Iceland, on the Russian steppes, and down near the spot where John Huss' body was burned in Prague. The descendants of the Hugenots read it under the shadow of the Tuilleries. It is read in the land of Cervantes, and the Arab, the Armenian, the

Argentine and the Greek may find life in its
pages. It is read in India, in Africa, in Mexico,
in the Fiji Islands, and has even been translated
for the benefit of the Cree Indians.

The blind may read it in Braille, and there
is no nation under the sun that does not know
its presence. After the missionary translates the
Bible he translates Pilgrim's Progress, and that
day when the last trump is sounded and the
heavens roll up like a scroll some sincere soul will
see with his latest earthly sight the pages of this
book.

Bunyan —
Teacher of Childhood

A committee headed by the Earl of Shafts-
bury put a beautiful statue over the grave of
Bunyan in Bunhill Fields in 1861. This recum-
bent statue is suggestive of the dreamer. In 1874,
June 10, an even more beautiful statue to his
memory was erected on St. Peter's green, Bedford. This was presented to the Borough of
Bedford by the Ninth Duke of Bedford. This
statue shows Bunyan standing with a book in
his hand. When the statue was unveiled Dean

Stanley of Westminster made the principal speech. This was significant for it showed that the good men in the Established Church were not in sympathy with the blind and mean persecution which had put a blot on their history. Certainly no one for a moment would blame the devout Christian souls in the Established Church for the foolishness of their fathers.

Perhaps no greater tribute was ever paid Bunyan than was paid him on this occasion when this man who stood in the very forefront of his Church in that great nation spoke glowingly of his genius and his goodness. There was one thing Dean Stanley said that deserves to be remembered. He spoke of Bunyan who was great as a man and as a preacher, but greater still "as the dear teacher of the childhood of each of us, as the creator of those characters whose names and faces are familiar to the whole world." I have no doubt but that you, reader, read Bunyan as a child, and you can say with the poet Cowper as you go gleaning down the fields of memory in the golden sunlight of later life,

"Oh thou, whom borne on fancy's eager wing,
Back to the season of Life's happy spring,

I pleased remember and while memory yet holds
Fast her office here can never forget.
Ingenious dreamer, in whose well-told tale
Sweet fiction and sweet truth alike prevail;
Whose humorous vein strong sense and simple
    style
May teach the gayest, make the bravest smile;
Witty and well employed, and like thy Lord,
Speaking in parables His slighted word."

" * * * Rather Than Thus to Violate My Faith and Principle"

And now, before we part, let us understand
each other. What I have been trying to do in
everything I have written is to make you see
Bunyan as a man of God. I am praying that
there may be a new birth in the lives of those who
would follow John Bunyan's Lord. We can
learn with profit a few things from the life of
this man. I wish we had something of his consecration, of his devotion to a cause; I wish we had
something of the same stuff in our system that
would make us love the Lord supremely, and
"reverence our conscience as our king."

I wish that instead of trying to side-step and live softly we would say as he said when they offered him liberty at the price of his convictions: "But if nothing will do, unless I make of my conscience a continual butchery and slaughter-shop, unless, putting out my own eyes, I commit me to the blind to lead me, as I doubt is desired by some, I have determined, the Almighty God being my help and shield, yet to suffer, if frail life might continue so long, even till the moss shall grow on mine eyebrows, rather than thus to violate my faith and principles."